Praise for *Three*

"For anyone who has struggled to establish a meditation practice — or, alternatively, isn't yet convinced they ought to try — this book offers an unusually simple and elegant way forward. Three minutes a day is much too short a period to trigger the usual resistance, yet it's easily enough to begin to experience the profound benefits of cultivating the mind."
— **Oliver Burkeman**, bestselling author of *Four Thousand Weeks: Time Management for Mortals*

"Richard Dixey effectively punctures the myth that meditation has to be a long, tedious slog. Instead, he offers a savory tasting menu of approaches and experiences. The changing flavors keep us interested, and the bite-size portions keep us encouraged that we really can do it."
— **Dean Sluyter**, author of *Natural Meditation* and *The Dharma Bum's Guide to Western Literature*

"Finally, a user-friendly owner's manual for the mind! This book takes you on a journey with engaging exercises that are perfectly paced, covers all the dos and don'ts of developing a meaningful meditation practice, and provides profound insights into the nature of mind. Written in such a clear and concise way, it will enrich beginning and experienced meditators alike."
— **Khandro Kunzang Dechen Chodron**, director of P'hurba Thinley Ling and Saraswati Publications

"Brilliant. With his years of experience, depth of understanding, and innate wisdom, Richard Dixey is able to take the reader on a meditation journey that is clear, strong, and transformative. This book is not to be gobbled but lived, with the author by your side as a friend and fine teacher. I loved it."

— **Victoria Riskin**,
president and publisher of *Bluedot Living*

Three
Minutes
a Day

Three Minutes a Day

A Fourteen-Week Course to
Learn **MEDITATION** and
Transform Your Life

Richard Dixey

New World Library
Novato, California

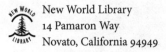 New World Library
14 Pamaron Way
Novato, California 94949

Text design by Tona Pearce Myers

Library of Congress Cataloging-in-Publication Data

Names: Dixey, Richard, author.
Title: Three minutes a day : a fourteen-week course to learn meditation and transform your life / Richard Dixey.
Description: Novato : New World Library, 2023. | Summary: "Details a 14-week course to develop a stable meditation practice that can be completed in less time than having a morning cup of coffee. Includes a series of 14 three-minute exercises, introduced by a brief description, and enriched by questions and answers"-- Provided by publisher.
Identifiers: LCCN 2023021250 (print) | LCCN 2023021251 (ebook) | ISBN 9781608688838 (paperback) | ISBN 9781608688845 (epub)
Subjects: LCSH: Buddhist meditations. | Meditation--Buddhism--Study and teaching.
Classification: LCC BQ5572 .D59 2023 (print) | LCC BQ5572 (ebook) | DDC 294.3/4435--dc23/eng/20230520
LC record available at https://lccn.loc.gov/2023021250
LC ebook record available at https://lccn.loc.gov/2023021251

First printing, August 2023
ISBN 978-1-60868-883-8
Ebook ISBN 978-1-60868-884-5
Printed in Canada on 100% postconsumer-waste recycled paper

 New World Library is proud to be a Gold Certified Environmentally Responsible Publisher. Publisher certification awarded by Green Press Initiative.

10   9   8   7   6   5   4   3   2   1

With deepest thanks to TT and DJKR

The aim of philosophy is to free our natural intelligence from its bewitchment by language.

Ludwig Wittgenstein

Contents

Preface

This book makes a bold claim:

Just three minutes a day, for fourteen weeks. That is a bit less than five hours. In this time, if you actually spend three minutes a day for fourteen weeks, you can generate a real insight into personal experience that no amount of reading can replicate.

SO
the deal is this: *Don't* read this book right through! It is very short, so it would be easy to do that.

RATHER
just read the introduction, read chapter 1, and then do the simple meditation, three minutes a day, for seven days.

THEN
read chapter 2. Do the simple meditation, three minutes a day, for seven days.

AND THEN

read chapter 3, do the simple meditation, three minutes a day, for seven days, and so on!

AT THE END,

if you do this, you will have yourself a base of experience upon which a house of insight can be built.

To help you, we have built an app called Three Minutes that is available for free through the iOS and Android app stores.

iOS   Android

Introduction

Since childhood, I have been fascinated by perception — what experience means to each of us personally. I realized in my late teens that almost all Western accounts of experience are predicated on being explained by someone else, as if experience itself could be expressed in the third person. I remember looking out on a city street with people walking along the pavement, and thinking that each one of them was in a bubble of their own, entirely unknowable to me. But I had a vague intuition that there was more to know, somewhere, if only I could find it. Early encounters with meditation and other paths to mind exploration soon came to dominate my interest, so I left my home in England and took off to India after my second year studying the sciences at university to see what I could discover.

Of course, I didn't find what I was looking for — not then, anyway. I remember sitting at the feet of a gray-haired pandit in orange robes on the edge of the lake promenade in Nainital, a somewhat incongruously English town in the Himalayan foothills. With a ferocious, glinting eye, he looked over the motley crew of Westerners I was part of, all of us on some quest or other. His gaze fell on me. Leaning forward, he pointed, jabbing his finger, and in almost a shout exclaimed, "You, you!! Go home!"

I didn't right away — I was far too stubborn. But a few months later I was back on a plane arriving into London. My intuition that there was something more was still intact, but my progress toward it was not so impressive. While finishing my degree, I came across the kabbalah and the hermetic esoteric tradition, and realized with a shock that great swaths of Western culture had been forced into the shadows by the triumphant march of empirical rationality. Was that where the secret lay? It wasn't long before some serious shortcomings with the esoteric traditions became apparent, though. If you have no standard of true knowledge, what is to stop you from merely making stuff up?

It's a dilemma. On the one hand, the proven techniques of empirical demonstration such as the scientific method lead to knowledge that others can replicate, but it is impersonal knowledge, not directly related to the knower. On the other hand, the seductive appeal of personal knowledge can open the door to all kinds of illusion and fantasy. In many ways the modern world is in the grip of these two currents, with no obvious way out.

Through a lucky series of events, I ended up running a research unit in a major London hospital, exploring some of the healing arts that special people can manifest. From there I observed the remarkable efficacy of certain traditional medicines. By what means had such extraordinary knowledge been generated? Was there another way of finding the truth of things?

So began a second career — scouring the world for traditional therapies and raising the funds to examine them in formal clinical studies. As chief executive of what became a well-known public company in the UK, again I experienced some successes, but trying to force these exquisite products of traditional culture into the mold of modern pharmaceuticals was no easier than researching the healing arts. The intuition that personal knowledge could be studied still stood, but what were the means?

All the time there was something in the background. There was one tradition with an unbroken, almost umbilical connection with antiquity that I had not properly looked at. I am referring of course to the meditation traditions of Asia, all of which span a thousand years, and some even longer, right back to 2,500 years ago, to a time when the means of knowing was very different from our own. Emphasizing learning, this culture created a tradition in which philosopher monks developed their knowledge, not only through logic and analysis, as our modern philosophers and scientists do, but also through their own meditation and personal development.

There it was! These practitioners had already squared the circle I had been orbiting, generating knowledge and insight from their own subjectivity while also submitting it to external scrutiny. Inspired by this, I caught the tail of the great influx of senior Tibetan instructors who came to Europe and America, and studied with them, along with Southeast Asian teachers who follow the Southern schools of equal antiquity. The more engaged I became, the more impressed I became — not only by the depth of the tradition that I had discovered, but by its extraordinary vastness and application.

In 2002 I had the great good fortune to meet my wife, Wangmo, the eldest daughter of a senior Tibetan lama. I decided to retire in 2007 and move with my young family to California, both to be close to Wangmo's parents and to devote myself to running a foundation in India, encouraging Theravadin monks to come back to India in large numbers, and Dharma College in Berkeley, California, where we live. Dharma College's mission is to present the ancient lineages of meditation and self-realization to a new audience, in a new language, and as part of that endeavor, I began teaching meditation classes there.

The task of translating my firsthand exposure to the meditation traditions and explaining them to a new audience led me to explore the themes in this book. A lot of what I have learned from many kind and patient teachers over the years has gone into the pages that follow. Some of the participants of my classes began transcribing them, and that is the origin of the text. Questions were asked, and I answered them as best I could; those questions and answers come at the end of each chapter. I introduce a handful of traditional terms from the Pali language of ancient India to give some points of reference, but I hope sincerely that I have been able to contextualize them so thoroughly that they have ceased to be technical and have become shorthand for the specific experiences that the short meditation sessions explore. Words serve to inform, but, in meditation perhaps more than any other activity, it is essential that the information becomes part of personal experience. Once it does, the words do not matter so much. Nonetheless, if you need a reminder of the meaning of any of these terms, you can look them up in the glossary at the back of the book.

As for how to do it, I prefer to meditate with my eyes open whenever I can, breathing normally, since developing faculties of mind with the senses open and without trying to manipulate the body lessens the difference between whatever we practice in our meditation sessions and our far more extensive post-meditation experience. But some beginners find it distracting to have

their eyes open. See what works for you. It is also helpful to sit in a chair, or on a cushion if it is comfortable,
with the aim of adopting a posture in which the body
can rest quietly and in balance, without needing adjust-
ment. Of course, one could do this lying down, but the
tendency then is to fall asleep!

The *Three Minutes a Day* approach was born out of
traditions that stress short and repeated meditation
exercises rather than long sessions of sitting. However,
this is not true of all schools, and there are many other
approaches. For me, I have found that the short-session
method forms a good foundation and makes it easy
to establish a meditation practice one can build upon
easily.

Meditation is a useful, perhaps even essential, element
of self-exploration, a practice that can develop a reliable foundation for both subjective knowledge and
emotional resilience. I hope that some of the readers of
this book will embark on it, as it is a rich and fulfilling
practice that can quietly enhance journaling, prayer,
contemplation, or any other element of a life well lived.
It will not end with these fourteen exercises, but they
can make a good start. For others, already exposed to
other meditation approaches, it may give a new perspective on what they are doing and feel like a breath
of fresh air. Finally, for still others, I hope I can show
that modern physiological and psychological insights
are entirely concordant with self-development in this

manner, and so in no way should meditation be seen as something alternative to a modern way of life.

To me, it is a useful skill — one that can open the door to an altogether richer way of being. Once we begin, there is no limit to the exploration that lies before us.

CHAPTER ONE

Nearly Struck by Lightning

Nowadays, because of security cameras, you can find all kinds of videos on the internet. If you search for "person struck by lightning," many come up. You'll see a flash, and when you slow down the video, you'll see the person struck fall like a log.

One 2019 video is a little different. Taken by a security camera in South Carolina, it shows a man hurrying along a walkway in the pouring rain. He is striding along, taking about two steps a second, hiding under his umbrella. About halfway across there is a huge flash, and then he doubles over, recovers himself, and runs away. You can see the video on YouTube here: www.youtube.com/watch?v=Hq6QojuQ6qA.

Slow it down, and something really important emerges. The video captures the actual moment when the lightning bolt hits the grass a few feet from him. In the next frame a huge flash whites out the entire screen.

But the next frame shows the man still walking, gait unchanged. He takes a whole step, almost half a second, before you see him doubling over, staggering, and then beginning to run for cover. So what happens in that half a second — that finger snap between actuality and experience, even when the actuality is as intense as nearly getting hit by lightning? This is what meditation helps us to examine.

Meditation has entered our common language. It's quite the vogue nowadays. We are told to "attend to the present," to "be here now," to "develop mindful awareness." Somehow the simple act of sitting quietly and watching something, normally the breath, brings all these benefits. But why? And how?

In this book, I attempt to answer these questions and present a selection of short but effective meditation practices that relate to the answers. In so doing, I hope to remove some of the preconceptions that make meditation an obsession for some — and a seemingly unattainable goal for many others.

Behind the Curve

Meditation is a skill. It's like learning to ski, knit, or play the violin. It's not a religious activity per se; it is a method of working with our own experience. Meditation is a way of doing something that in modern times we generally don't often do, which is to look at our own experience *as experience*. Meditation helps us to hold back from merely looking through our experience at "things" we identify outside ourselves, or reacting to thoughts and feelings that might arise in our inner world. Rather, it enables us to look at our experience itself.

We're not used to doing this, so it takes a little practice.

This new skill of learning to look at our own experience produces inner resilience, the ability to deal with challenge and stress more effectively. Now, why would it produce inner resilience? This question is really a key to the whole issue of meditation. What comes next is a surprise initially and then sinks in as a piece of obvious common sense. It is the realization that our experience is constructed. Our experience is generated from our sense impressions and is the result of many rapidly unfolding processes scientists have been studying for over a century. But what do we know about such activity?

Many of us were taught in school that the three dimensions we see with our eyes are actually a construct, made from differences between the images processed in one eye compared with the other. Depth as an experience is a creation of our sense apparatus. In a similar manner, our ability to locate the source of sounds that we hear is computed from phase differences between the sound arriving in one ear and the other. Modern experiments and discoveries, like the phenomenon of phantom limbs experienced by amputees, for example, show that our body image is equally a construct. Indeed, this is quite generally the case with all our sense inputs; all our experience is constructed. But how? Can we gain access to direct experience without these layers of construction?

Meditation can help us answer this question. It can help us understand the display or map in which we live. This statement is not an attempt to make arm-waving metaphysical claims about the world, that it doesn't exist or anything like that. It is simply pointing out something pretty obvious: we all have a *reaction time*. A reaction time is the time it takes us to react to something. It's what we experience when we see a glass falling to the floor and attempt to reach it with our hand but miss it. But as the lightning video shows us, all our experiences happen within a reaction time, and that reaction time is actually quite long. It means we are effectively one finger snap behind reality, behind whatever is happening at the time, all the time.

So let's return to our question. What happens in that finger snap between an event and our reaction to it? What lies there? The practice of meditation reveals that in that gap lies something really important. In that gap of a little under half a second it takes for us to experience anything, our experience is configured, colored, influenced, not only by our sense inputs, but also by what we believe and all the experiences we have had, good and bad. Those influences make us who we are. The problem is, that configured experience is something we then react to, receiving it as if it is the world itself. We react to the display we ourselves have created as if it is unreservedly real, actually the case. This blindness to our own situation is why we find ourselves so often feeling nervous, feeling uncomfortable, feeling out of sorts and not really knowing why. Often we find ourselves triggered by things, and we don't know the reason. Our blindness to all that unconscious, reflexive reactivity is a profound source of stress.

If we can learn how reactivity occurs and how we might get a handle on it, we develop resilience, become more flexible, and learn to deal with situations as they are rather than merely reacting to them. We become more accommodating. This is not the same as becoming unresponsive; rather, it is developing the ability to understand our reactivity and hence reduce it. This is one of the great fruits of meditation.

Shamata and Vipassana

The practice of meditation has two elements. The first one is calmness meditation. It's called *shamata* in the Pali language of old India, where it was developed. You can think of *shamata* like this: You have a glass of water. It's full of chalk dust or fine mud, so when you stir it up, the water's all cloudy and turbulent. You can't see through it at all. But if you put the glass down on a table and wait, over time all the dust and mud particles settle. Eventually all that is left is clear water with a sediment on the bottom. This process of settling is very similar to *shamata*. *Shamata* is about learning to leave things alone, not to react, not to stir up the mud and cloud our vision. *Shamata* meditation sessions are about reducing reactivity so that our psychology is not being wound up all the time, reacting to events that arise in our constructed experience. It is a skill we can learn in a surprisingly short amount of time, as long as we know exactly what we're doing.

As with learning any skill, it's important to understand the instrument we are working with, our own mind. This incredible instrument is the one within which we were born and within which we will die. Honestly, it would be wonderful if we were all born with an instruction manual, but as it is, we come into the world and have to make it up as we go along! So how can we usefully describe our experience? We could say our mind has six inputs, like a six-channel parallel processor: an input for each of the five senses, and an input for our thoughts and feelings. Or we could say the mind is like a city with six gates: again, one gate for each of the five senses and another for thoughts and feelings. These gates are the six channels of experience.

What happens in our cognitive process is that our attention is directed to inputs at one or another of the gates from moment to moment, depending on how important we find it. The sense of importance that causes us to pay attention to one gate or another is often related to threat. If our senses detect a formation that seems to be a threatening pattern, our attention is switched to that sense gate. This unconscious reactivity is what causes the sense of pervasive disquiet we so often experience.

It is difficult to address all six gates at the same time. So in order to reduce our reactivity, many meditation techniques simplify our experience by focusing on one of the gates and asking us to ignore the other five. This enables us to control our reactivity more effectively with reference to a single channel, rather than to all six. The effect is to quiet all our senses. If we're able to reduce reactivity in one of the gates, it makes all of them less reactive. So the dust and mud begin to settle in the glass; the water of our experience begins to clarify; and we begin to see clearly.

That clarity, in the ancient language of India, is called *vipassana*. *Passana* means "seeing," and *vi* means "discriminating" or "clear" — "clear seeing." This is the other element of meditation. Clear seeing is the fruit of calmness. We can see clearly when all the dust and mud have settled in a glass of water. So *vipassana* is the fruit of *shamata*. Put another way, until we have *shamata*, *vipassana* is not possible, because the water is so cloudy we can't see anything at all.

EXERCISE
Watching a Candle

It is time to inquire how we can begin to approach the practice of *shamata*. As long as we understand what we are doing, and do it single-mindedly, three minutes a day is enough. To work with this book is to make a promise that we'll try the exercises for three minutes a day. That's all. If we are really ambitious, we can do three minutes twice a day, perhaps morning and evening, but really all that's required is three minutes once a day. For this week's practice, the key is to have a clear intention and a good understanding that what we are doing is limiting our experience to one of the sense gates and focusing on that.

We can start by using our familiar faculty of concentration, something we have been taught to do from our earliest childhood, to focus on one sense gate to the exclusion of the others. This is a famous meditation technique. It's called *trataka* in the old yogic tradition. *Trataka* can be done with any sensation, such as a sound or touch, but vision is generally our most dominant gate, so it makes sense to start there. One of the most accessible ways to do it is to watch a candle flame. Of course, one can use any sense input in this manner, be it hearing, tasting, touching, feeling, or indeed, thoughts. The key is to select one sense gate and follow it.

What we do is light a candle and focus our eyes on the flame for three minutes. It quivers and moves, and every now and then our concentration will also waver. We just bring our attention back to watching the flame. It is actually good that the candle flame is slightly moving. With a static object, like a statue or something, one tends to glaze over and lose focus because nothing's happening; it's not engaging enough. That blankness is not concentrated attention.

Choose any candle you like. Put it about six inches away. Sit comfortably. A straight back is good so that you are stable and not leaning one way or another. Then rest your gaze on the candle flame. Every time your concentration wanders off, bring it back.

By doing this we are gradually educating our attentive capacity, telling it that we want it to rest on this object. There is no need to provide any further rationale — that we are doing it for this reason or that. We just watch.

Whenever a thought comes or a sound happens, it attracts our attention to another gate. All we do is merely turn back and place our attention on the flame again. If we can do this for three minutes a day for the next seven days, it will create the basis for the next step.

You could say that successful *shamata* is when our concentration has become so stable and effortless that it is not disturbed by anything. Our mind becomes flexible, calm, and compliant, able to rest on any object we choose without worry or aversion. And that's one of the goals we are working toward.

Five Obstacles

There are five obstacles that immediately begin to manifest when we do something like this. In meditation manuals, they are called the five *nivaranas*, or the five hindrances. They come in two pairs, plus an odd one.

The first pair is agitation and dullness. Agitation is what many of us begin to notice when we sit quietly. A sea of agitation is churning beneath our normal awareness. This chatter is the first insight into our mental apparatus. Our minds are always working away, taking inputs from our senses, comparing them to past experiences, and projecting future outcomes. As such, this activity has high value in terms of human cognition and evolution, even if it is a source of stress. This remarkable capacity allows us to learn from experience and use those memories to guide our future actions. It has taken a lowly ape and, over the eons, elevated it into a position of world domination. But when we begin to rest the mind, all this activity suddenly becomes apparent. It's actually going on all the time. We just don't notice it.

As we bring our attention back to the candle flame, sometimes the opposite manifests, and we become sleepy or dull. Dullness is the next obstacle; it's as if we have suddenly become exhausted. Again, the trick is not to resist too strongly. We patiently bring our attention back to the candle flame. It's only three minutes, after all!

The second pair of obstacles manifests as two types of disturbing thoughts. The first is when we wander off into daydreams of things that attract us — things we want or desire. The second is when we wander off into thinking about things we want to avoid or change. But with this wandering tendency that manifests as the *nivaranas* of attraction and aversion, too, we can be patient. These fantasies are normal activity — planning and imagining scenarios — that goes on all the time.

Finally, as we bring our attention back, the last *nivarana* manifests. It is doubt — the final obstacle to any change. "Why should I do this?" we say to ourselves. "What is the point?" When this happens, we simply have to take back the reins of our attention and rest it on the object, in this case, the candle, without providing explanations or debating with ourselves. It's like the Nike slogan — just do it!

Questions and Comments

Is the final *nivarana*, doubt, something like "Why am I doing this? I have better things to do?"

Yes. It's "Why am I bothering?" It comes up much more later on. It is the ultimate *nivarana*. You could argue, "There's a real world out there. We've got nuclear weapons. We've got good mobile phones. Why bother doing this?" That doubt is a very powerful impulse, behind which lies the gate to wisdom.

When doing this exercise, I've found that I can focus my attention on the flame in different ways. For example, I can outline it, stare at it, or follow the different lines

formed by its wavering. Or should I just gaze at it in an unfocused way?

A gaze leads to one of the *nivaranas*: it tends to drift into a drowsiness. You don't want to gaze; rather, look at the flame. You can examine it if you like, but not so that you make a commentary. You're going to get a lot of resistance from your six-channel parallel processor, which will try to look hard, or examine, or space out. Try to avoid that. Look. Stay with the object, without any other intention.

It is easier to stay with an object and not fall asleep or get distracted if it's an object I'm interested in. For example, I was looking at pictures of lakes and streams, and I found it easier to focus on them. I get distracted more easily with the candle flame.

You're getting fooled by your mental apparatus. We're not trying to be interested. All we're trying to do is rest our attention on a chosen object. This is a first step. We say to our mental apparatus, "Stop here. Do that and nothing more." It is always going to give us its little game. Instead of resting in attention, we often enter a commentary about the object. The object ceases to exist, and the commentary consumes us. We'll talk about this in the sessions to come. For now, keep returning your attention to the candle flame.

Only read on once you have done
your seven days!

CHAPTER TWO

Overcoming Brittleness

We live in a culture that stresses concentration. All of us have had years of schooling where the teacher said, "Concentrate! Don't be distracted!" The school examination system emphasizes this ability to narrowly focus and concentrate on the task at hand. That kind of concentration is what we're used to employing to get things done. When we try to rest our mind on an object, we tend to concentrate on that object. We think being mindful is concentrating. We think that the injunction "be here now" is really about concentrating on the here and now so that nothing escapes our attention.

Concentration like this is brittle. That's to say, when we concentrate on one thing, other things take our concentration away. Classically, thoughts take our concentration away, so when we try to concentrate on a candle flame, thoughts come up and we have to remind ourselves that we're concentrating on the candle flame and return to it. Even if we manage to conquer thoughts, external noises take our concentration away — someone slams a car door or starts a pneumatic drill or plays some music. This feeling of concentration being brittle, of its tendency to be disturbed easily, is a very common experience.

If our concentration is brittle, we are unlikely to be able to deepen it very far before something comes along and disrupts it. We live in a contingent world full of other people, and before we know it, we're being disturbed by some sound or some event that is outside our control. Indeed, one of the major misconceptions about calmness meditation, *shamata*, is that it is merely concentrated meditation.

There is a way to approach this issue. The early meditators classified concentration into two phases, and this analysis is very helpful. The first phase is called *vitaka*, and the second, *vicara*. *Vitaka* is the faculty of mind that enables us to pay attention to something; that is to say, to advert our attention — to move it toward something. Indeed, that is where the word *advertising* comes from. Advertising makes you advert your attention, capturing it. So *vitaka* is the ability to focus on something deliberately. This is a bit like our normal understanding of concentration, except it is slightly more technical.

The second phase is *vicara*. *Vicara* is the ability to savor the object you have adverted to. So it's a bit like you take a piece of chocolate and put it in your mouth, and the initial reaction is "Oh, it's chocolate!" That's *vitaka*. *Vicara* is to then taste the chocolate, to enjoy the experience. The chocolate is in your mouth, you've turned toward it, you are concentrated — but now you savor the chocolate. That second phase is an extended experience — it isn't immediate.

Vitaka is lifting the cup of coffee to your lips. *Vicara* is savoring the aroma and feeling that caffeinated tingle as we take our first sips. This is where many of us can go in the wrong direction. Having focused on an object of attention, we no longer stay with that object. We replace it with an idea of the object. So instead of savoring the object, we fix the object. We gulp down our coffee, scoff our food, almost without tasting it. We get an out-of-focus feeling, as if we can't hold the object in our visual or sensory field. It begins to blur as our adverted attention becomes exhausted and we begin to slip into a distracting commentary or reaction to it. If we're stuck in *vitaka*, without the engaged attention of *vicara*, we lose contact with the original sensation altogether.

You could also say *vitaka* is like hitting something and *vicara* is the object vibrating after it's been struck. A classic example is a bell. Striking the bell is *vitaka*, and the ringing sound that it makes is *vicara*. The word *vicara* designates our capacity to hold attention on a changing object. Putting our attention on the object is *vitaka*, but *vicara* is the capacity to hold our attention there. Now, of course, if it's the fading sound of a bell, what we are doing is listening to the sound as it fades. We are not being distracted by the fading but are staying with it, and eventually, of course, the sound fades into silence. But we are still attending to it.

This capacity to hold attention on a moving object is what removes the brittleness from concentration. Indeed, once we can hold attention on a fading object we find calm spaciousness within concentration itself. Our concentration is no longer dependent on having an object to concentrate on. You might say that we have made a transition from following a fading sensation to being focused and attentive as a state in itself.

This transition from *vitaka* to *vicara* is an important development that broadens our base of meditation. Other sensations can arise within that savoring concentration, but instead of having either concentration on some object or distraction by another, which is how we normally operate, we can enter *vicara*, the state in which we can be concentrated without an object at all. When another sound arises, it arises within our concentration, not as an alternative to it.

If we can make this transition, we can ride the horse of concentrated attention. We can create a stable base of calmness. The calm state becomes a state in which events occur but don't distract us. And they don't distract us because we've moved our *vitaka* into *vicara*, into a state of calm concentration.

Although this faculty of calm concentration is extraordinarily valuable, it's not identified clearly in Western culture very much. Of course, you hear athletes talking about getting "in the zone," and that is much the same idea. Competitors enter a state of concentration, and if it is stable, other things don't distract them. Naturally, some athletes struggle with the zone, which is why you hear them getting upset if the crowd makes noises or some small thing happens they don't like, and they struggle with this transition. But nonetheless, the idea of the zone is very similar. You could say in meditation we're trying to become accomplished athletes or skilled artisans of our own perception. And the zone we want to get into is that zone of calm, so instead of being reactive to our sense gates all the time and thrown out of kilter, we end up calmly centered in what's happening around us.

A second feature of this distinction between *vitaka* and *vicara* concerns effort. Initially *vicara* can be quite fleeting. We begin to realize that as we drop our focused attention, which is an act of will, and start to savor, which is an act of engagement, we lose focus very quickly. We are used to effort, and when we don't exercise it, we drift off into distraction. But in many ways the savoring that is the feature of *vicara* is to go beyond effort; it is to enter into a relationship with what is arising. You don't have to make an effort to taste chocolate. You might need to pick up a piece of chocolate and put it in your mouth, but once it's in your mouth, it's effortless. It's that quality of *vicara* that we are looking for. It is engagement itself.

Initially, when we exercise *vicara*, it rapidly disintegrates into distraction. That's to be expected. Rather than feel frustrated by this, we go back and place our attention on the meditation object again, then relax and allow our experience of ourselves and the meditation object to be one together. It's a bit like dancing in the old-fashioned sense, when you are in contact with someone else. As you move together to the music, you become a uniform entity wherein both of you enter a state of *vicara*. The other person's movement and your movement are linked together, and you're savoring the experience. That is why it is such a pleasant feeling. You go from an initial moment of contact into engagement.

Merely being focused on a meditation object always leads to brittleness because subjects change, events change, and when they do, the depth of concentration is affected. That's why many meditators say they can only meditate when they are on their meditation cushion. And the moment they get off their cushion, it's gone. Then how do they get their meditation back? They have to get on their cushion again! But honestly, that's kind of useless. They end up having to meditate eight hours a day, maybe even ten hours. I've met people like this at meditation retreats. "I meditate twenty hours!" "I meditated for fifty hours last week!" — that kind of stuff. Maybe there's a problem with one's meditation if one has to sit on a cushion so long.

EXERCISE
The Sound of a Fading Bell

This week we use a bell or a gong and allow its sound to fade into silence. Having given our attention to the bell as we strike it, we stay with the sound as it fades away. In so doing, our concentration becomes formless. We no longer concentrate on anything. We relax the focus of our concentration so that the concentration is not brittle. It is not brittle because it is not predicated on a fixed object. We then have a state of concentration that is flexible and can't be easily disturbed.

If you have a bell or a gong or any reverberating object, use it. Strike it and then stay with the fading sound. If you don't have a bell, the internet is full of recordings. So by all means, use those. They will also work. Stay with the sound as it fades and experience your ability to do so. You can then rest in silence for a bit until you get distracted, and then ring the bell or play the sound again.

Do this for three minutes a day. You'll end up striking the bell a few times, but as you get used to it, you will find yourself concentrated in silence for steadily longer periods. It's transitioning from *vitaka*, adverted attentiveness, into *vicara*, savoring attentiveness. Making that transition opens the door to all kinds of other transformations we can then make to broaden the platform of calmness we are creating.

Becoming Flexible

When a disturbance happens, we say it "breaks" our concentration. In using such a word, we are confirming the brittle nature of concentration. What would happen if our attention were more spacious? Disturbances could then occur within the state of attention, not as invading alternatives to it. This is important. Far from being disturbances, in such a state arising events are transformed into components of the object of attention itself. For this reason, the transition from *trataka* (meditation on a single object, such as a candle flame) to *vitaka-vicara* is very valuable. Indeed, making this transition overcomes a major obstacle to developing a stable meditation practice: our meditation becomes totally portable. We're no longer obligated to sit on our meditation cushion. We can use our increasing faculty where it belongs, which is in our actual experience, rather than developing a special subset of our life experience in the morning or on special days of the year — in other words, whenever we engage in a formal meditation practice.

Questions and Comments

If you work with a bell, what should you do after the bell stops ringing?

Keep listening to the silence after the sound fades away. When you find that you can't hang there in silence, ring the bell again. That's fine too. This is a dance. We're learning how to dance, dance with *vitaka* and *vicara*.

What I noticed as it was fading is that other sounds were kind of coequal. I'm assuming I want to try to keep the bell sound in the foreground, even though the other sounds that impinge might be louder at that moment in my auditory field. So should we try to shut out the others as the sound of the bell is fading? Should we try to stay with the diminishing sound and not attend to things coming from elsewhere?

Once you've established the ability to stay with the fading sound, by all means allow other sounds to become objects, which you also stay with. You don't have to stay with the one bell sound as if there were something magical about it. You can go to another sound and let that one fade. What we are doing with *vicara* is allowing ourselves to savor experience, without selecting out of experience any particular element. We suddenly realize that all experiences are equal. What makes them different is the way we respond to them.

When you start recognizing that, *vicara* becomes a key to the equality, the sameness of experience, and everything ends up on the same level, as something to savor. This is why it's such an important faculty. So as an initial exercise, it's valuable to follow the fading sound. But once we've become familiar with resting on this changing sound, then we can allow any other sounds to come in. This yields a much broader base for calmness.

When I am dealing with *vitaka-vicara* I feel like I sink down into my body and out of my head. Is this common?

Yes. A lot of cultures teach that the center of our being is actually our heart, not our head. This awareness is an aspect of becoming embodied. In fact, to describe what we're aiming for, you could use the word *embodiment* and completely ditch the word *meditation*. But the word *embodiment* has its own connotations. Whatever word you use is going to be wrong in one aspect or another. In any case, yes, this practice involves shifting from ideation into sensation, and that movement has a downward feel to it.

Could we use chocolate for our meditations?

Yes, I guess so, if you want to eat bars of chocolate. That's a pretty cool idea! You can use any sense gate. You could use the sensation of silk on your fingers, or of a feather brushing against your face. It doesn't matter which sense gate you use.

Meditation is not about the sense gate; it's about our reaction to it. So, yes, eat chocolate if you want to! I think after a while you might get bored of putting chocolate in your mouth and tasting it. But you know, if you eat prodigious quantities of it, why not? That could work. Any sensation can be used as an object of *shamata*. Any one of the gates. Ultimately we're going to look at thought itself. That is the ultimate meditation object. But to get to being able to look at thought requires us to develop faculties of mind that most of us haven't experienced.

We get distracted by thoughts so we can't look at them. But in time the capacity to look directly at thoughts will develop, and to do that, of course, is to become aware of the most powerful gate of all.

With all of that said, the auditory sense gate, via the sound of a bell, is an accessible one that most of us find very easy to use.

Only read on once you have done
your seven days!

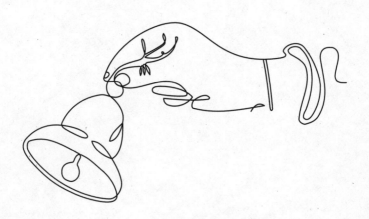

CHAPTER THREE

Turning to Touch

In every moment of experience, we are generating a display, a readout that makes sense of what we receive via our sensory inputs. This is the primary function of our cognitive apparatus. Think back to the guy nearly hit by lightning mentioned in the opening chapter. The moment that elapsed between when the lightning struck and when he began to react is the period in which the display is generated. Of course, that initial response may not have been fully conscious, and ripples of it, in terms of reactions arising from a narrative of what happened, would surely have extended far, far longer; but nonetheless, the readout is continuous, moment to moment, emerging in that short gap after the sensations that trigger it.

Ultimately this readout-generating activity will become a major element of interest in our practice of meditation. Difficulties arise for us because this process of making sense of the world contains not merely elements based on the best guess of what our senses tell us, but also multiple colorants based on our previous experiences, beliefs, and upbringing. This is why becoming aware of how we generate the display can lead to greater resilience when things do not unfold the way we expect.

Developing *vitaka* is a big step in this direction, even if it is brittle. By developing a capacity to direct our attention, we begin to overcome the instant reactivity that we otherwise experience, where our attention is adverted to this thing or that, without our capacity to control it. But once we begin to enter the dance of *vicara*, savoring our experience rather than merely reacting to it, something of a different order begins to manifest. We begin to exhaust clear-cut expectations and outcomes, and enter a relationship with the flow of events themselves. So the attraction of *vicara* is that when it is properly developed, instead of distractions taking us away from our objects of attention, they become incorporated into our concentration. The distractions become another aspect of *vicara*. For example, if you are savoring your dinner, it doesn't matter if another taste arrives; you merely savor that as well. Your attention will no longer be brittle.

In every moment of our lived experience there is something beneath it that can be properly termed *primordial*. That is to say, at the beginning of each sensation, events happen before our internal stamping of *past* or *present* and without any judgment or assessment at all. A good example is when something shocks us. Just for an instant, after such an event, we experience a brief moment of clarity without any content at all. To notice such moments is to begin to see the display re-establishing itself and providing a narrative of what happened. To become aware of such a process is to discover a form of knowledge that truly pervades all aspects of our existence.

The classic vehicle for *vitaka* and *vicara* is breath meditation. This is sometimes called mindfulness meditation. It is a *shamata* meditation in which we bring our attention to a continuously moving object. Instead of the flickering of a candle or the fading of a bell, we attend to the sensation of the breath moving in and out. *Vitaka* brings attention to the sensation, normally the very slight sensation of the breath entering and leaving the nostrils or the rising and falling of the belly or chest. The *vicara* element is to stay with it and not lose interest. If we stay with the sensation, the object changes as we exhaust any preconception of what we are doing. One might say we begin to "get beneath" the idea of the breath to actual sensation itself.

What we're really looking for is a faculty of mind that might enable us to see our own state as it evolves in time, as it changes, as things happen to us. For that we must develop *vicara*. Otherwise we will never make it, and we'll end up sitting rigidly on a meditation cushion. If that is the case, as long as we can hold the rigid posture it's OK, but the moment we get up, it's all gone! Of course, once we're up everything is continuously changing, and our brittle concentration can't deal with it. This is rather humorously expressed by statues of the Buddha. Meditation is associated with the Buddha, and he is usually depicted sitting, very formally. But what about a statue of the Buddha brushing his teeth, or having lunch? The histories show he did those things, but we have no images of them! The problem is us; we have a static conception of what meditation should be about.

We normally don't access this more spacious experience of concentration because we react immediately to what is presented to us, and since this happens with every rising sensation, most of us have rarely experienced anything outside our known and cataloged set of experiences that arise in those reactions. We call this catalog "the world," and we find ourselves in it. As mentioned above, unless a catastrophic or totally unexpected event happens to us, in which case we get a brief moment of shock, we never experience anything else. Even after such an interruption, our "world" rapidly reconstructs itself. We're so unused to having direct experience without a catalog of known things that it is almost as if we cannot deal with it. But what would it be like to have an alternative, a cognizant awareness without the fixed structures of self and other, and without the three times of past, present, and future? All of us have glimpses of such a way of being — perhaps moved

by great beauty or some overwhelming experience —
but these moments are fleeting, seemingly beyond our
control. Meditation is a practice to develop an ability to
approach such experiences, and to stay there.

So in this phase of our meditation journey we are creating a platform from which we can move beyond static
models. We have to create a safe space to do this. We
are fragile. If we go beyond what we know, we are taking a risk, for we are going into the unknown. Our psychology, which is designed to keep us alive and safe, is
not going to approve of such an action without some
kind of negotiation. After all, it has gotten us this far.
We have learned what is good and what is bad from
past experience and training, and our inner intelligence will provide us information as a default to stop us
from doing dangerous things. We can only go beyond
this safe space through a process of negotiation with
our own psychology, to persuade it that it is safe to go
beyond this recognitive bubble that gives us a world of
known things. It is not normal to go beyond this point,
so our inner urges often hint, "This is unnatural. You
shouldn't be doing this." This innate caution is one of
the main drivers of doubt that we all experience. But
again, we can be patient and understand this concern.
Our task is to make steady, incremental progress, not
to go jumping off into some potentially hazardous and
unknown situation.

EXERCISE
The Sensation of the Breath

We began by looking at a candle, and then we moved on to listening to a fading bell. The candle worked with the eye gate, and the bell worked with the sound gate. Now we are going to change gates again and work with the gate of touch. You could, of course, merely feel the weight of your body on a chair. That would be a perfectly legitimate meditation object, but because it does not change much, maintaining awareness of it beyond initial contact is difficult.

What's attractive about the breath? Because we keep breathing, it provides a steadily changing object of meditation, which we can use as an object in *vitaka* and *vicara* practice. There are two sensations that happen while we're breathing. If we slightly close our mouths, the first one we can feel is the sensation of the air as it enters and leaves our nostrils near the tip of our nose. A second sensation is the feeling of our chest or belly expanding and contracting as we breathe. Either of these sensations is a perfectly good object for meditation.

Just as with the candle and the bell, for a period of three minutes, strongly turn your attention to this sensation of breathing, to the exclusion of other sensations or events happening at other sense gates. This is a classic *vitaka* exercise. Normally we are encouraged to meditate like this with our eyes closed so that no other sense inputs are active. We sit in a silent room to shut off auditory sensations.

Having established contact with the sensation of the breath, we then then follow it. That is *vicara*. Following the breath in and out without any special manner of breathing, we can develop *vicara* and expand concentration into an ever-widening base of awareness. We allow the savoring of the sensation of breathing to be continuous, a topic we will return to later on.

Learning to Be Effortless

Breathing is a powerful and classical meditation object. So in our three minutes, we take the sensation either between the nostrils or in our belly or chest, or wherever we can feel our body moving against our clothing. There's no particular reason to favor one sensation over the other. It might either be the cool touch of air on the nose or perhaps a slight feeling of movement as the fabric grazes the chest or a muscle expands and contracts in the belly. There are all kinds of different sensations that we are completely unaware of while we breathe, so it could be any one of a number of different sensations. It does not matter. All that matters is we choose one, turn our attention to it, and then savor it. And we do only that for three minutes.

Now, of course, the same instruction applies when thoughts come up. As was mentioned in chapter 1, they will be one of the five hindrances — daydreams triggered by either agitation, dullness, attraction, aversion or doubt. One can even think of them as our habitual "mapmaker" checking that everything is OK. In any case, once we notice they have arisen, we stop, reattend, re-establish *vicara*, and don't fight with them. There is no point. After all, the very thought of using effort to be undistracted in the face of such distractions is already a distraction! The very effort we make to meditate is itself not meditation. But it is only for three minutes, so we can be patient with it.

Meditation is learning to be effortless. This means that the sensation that's already there is our meditation object; we don't do anything apart from savor and stay with it. So when a moment of distraction arises and we find ourselves flying away on our mapmaker's magic carpet, wheeling through scenario after scenario of agitation, dullness, attraction, aversion, and doubt, we stop, reapply *vicara*, and stay there. Our breath will not have gone anywhere! We learn not to fight with distractions, because that fighting is another aspect of the magic carpet. It is totally pointless.

If we keep it up for three minutes, it doesn't matter how many times we are distracted. What will happen is our mental and physical system will get used to this activity, and slowly the distractions will become less and less pronounced. Most of them are caused by fear, fear of the unknown, and so they begin to subside as our mapmaker gets used to this unfamiliar activity. As we become comfortable with the practice, gradually we are able to hold our *vicara* for longer periods. Eventually our practice becomes effortless, so when the kinds of distractions arise that would normally break our concentration, they are merely smoothly incorporated into that calm clarity that we've steadily established. Once that has happened, they cease to be distractions; they become features of our calm clarity itself.

Now that, of course, is the end state that creates the stability we're working toward, a state one could call imperturbability. But it is not imperturbable like a statue. It is imperturbable because it incorporates every distraction into itself and hence has no opposition. There is nothing that can knock it off its perch.

Questions and Comments

I did three minutes twice a day, which makes six minutes.

Of course, we can meditate as long as we like. But if we stick with three minutes daily, the main thing is that we do it very deliberately. We are not just resting. It is possible to rest in meditation, but the danger is to merely sleep.

This practice is a little harder than watching the candle or listening to the fading bell, but it seems better because I can do it anywhere and nothing external is needed.

Breathing happens on its own, so we do not have to do anything to incite this phenomenon. But it is nonetheless an internal sensation rather than an external phenomenon that we are considering, so it is an excellent meditation object. The idea is to begin to introduce flexibility into our application of *vitaka* and *vicara*. But there is nothing to suggest that the earlier meditation objects of the bell and candle are worse, necessarily. You may find you get better results with an external object, at least initially. You do not have to limit yourself.

Remember always that *vicara* trick. Whenever anything comes to disturb you, engage with it for a moment, and then bring your attention back to your original object. You can become very relaxed. It's not a matter of being resistant. Once we understand *vicara*, we can flow.

I've been taught that if a thought comes up, we label it as a thought, but I have always found that to be a little disruptive. Are you saying we don't need the label — we can simply drop the thought?

There are different traditions. Choosing to say, "thought, thought" when a thought arises is one way of getting control. But that is not this technique. Here, as you point out, we simply go with it for a bit, then drop it and go back to the meditation object. Thoughts are always going to sneak up on us; we will always find ourselves attending to them. Some traditions say, "Return straightaway to your meditation object," but I think it is a little better simply to relax, drop the thought, and then return to your meditation. Otherwise there is a danger that you'll end up fighting with your thoughts to become what's called a "good meditator," which is itself a thought! So my advice is to engage with it, relax, drop it, and restart. It's like a dance. We are learning how to dance, very gradually, and after a while, the annoying thoughts disappear. They just do.

Can distractions also be emotions?

Yes, they can, but as you develop your *shamata* practice, you will notice that for every emotion there is always a thought or sensation that triggers it. Emotionality is always preceded by some kind of apprehension, at the heart of which lies a triggering idea. These ideas are sometimes called "loaded vectors" — charged apprehensions that attract memories and feelings, sometimes arising from long ago. Increasingly research is confirming that emotions are learned, arising in response to something that happened to us. So emotionality and thought are very, very close, and one of the aims of *shamata* is to be stable enough that when emotions arise, instead of being swept away by them, our stability enables us to see them. And when we do, we can see what triggered them. This gives us a handle on emotionality, which is normally an out-of-control experience; that handle is a major element of resilience.

Only read on once you have done
your seven days!

CHAPTER FOUR

Moving to the Mind Gate

In this stage of our meditation journey, we are developing and expanding our capacity for calm clarity. In the first week, we began by relying on an external anchor, initially a candle, that we could take as an object of focused concentration. In the second week, by examining why our focused concentration is so brittle, we identified two aspects within it, that of directing (*vitaka*) and savoring (*vicara*). We then began working with a changing external object, namely the sound of a bell as it fades into silence, learning to exercise *vicara* and so to stabilize concentration with a moving object. In the third week, we applied this skill of staying with a changing sensation to an omnipresent yet normally ignored sensation of touch, namely the touch of the air moving through the nose as we breathe in and out, or of our abdomen moving as our lungs expand and contract. Now, in this fourth week, we move our attention again, but this time onto an internally generated meditation object.

Alongside this steady exploration of the sensations that arise at one of the six gates of experience, we have also been generating direct experience of the five varieties of obstacle — the *nivaranas* — that arise in the process of meditation. The list falls into two pairs — agitation and dullness; attraction and aversion — plus doubt. It is very striking that even with only three minutes of meditation, we can have these kinds of experiences.

When one of the *nivaranas* manifests, it is a sign that we are beginning to focus on our actual experience, rather than living in a map of it as we normally do. Often we ignore these internal phenomena, which is why we can find ourselves with a sense of disquiet that can grow during the day. Sometimes we say, "I got up on the wrong side of the bed this morning!" What is really happening is that we are suppressing internal phenomena and just pushing through them in order to fulfill our everyday aims.

We have to do this to some extent, to get on with life, to make a living. There are lots of reasons why we learned to do this. But our meditation practice is pointing us in a different direction. For the short periods that we dedicate to this activity, what we are aiming to do is to engage totally with all of our experience, so that none of it is left unattended. One might almost say that meditation, or mind training, is really a means to explore our embodiment. We are learning to inhabit our own experience. Often meditation is described as if it is exclusively the practice of self-observation, as if our internal processes were somehow separate from us, but recognizing that self-observation and embodiment are referring to the same process can bring a lot of clarity to what we are doing.

In any case, the *nivaranas* play a big role. They are often called "obstacles" to meditation, but the word *obstacle* is actually not that helpful. When we seek embodied calmness rather than a brittle concentration that tries to push through or suppress other elements of our experience, we are beginning to develop a smooth reciprocity between what arises at our sense gates and our awareness of those sensations — the dance of *vicara* that we talked about earlier. As we do so, little wrinkles start to manifest — little misalignments that trigger stress responses. We are not used to being totally unified without some internal commentary. Perhaps an itch manifests, or a slight ache in the shoulders. Even if they are barely perceptible, such sensations often trigger a reaction — to want it or try to avoid it, or to shoot off into some digression or doubt, or to drift off into sleepiness. That is perhaps a better way to understand what the *nivaranas* are all about.

The technique to deal with these features is to roll with them, a bit like the famous judo throw in Japanese martial arts where you fall over as your opponent attacks you, and pull them over with you. If dullness manifests and you want to go to sleep, go to sleep; but give your-self permission to do so. When you accept rather than reject or resist feelings in this manner, the *nivarana*'s power to distract you evaporates. If you feel agitated, then shake your limbs, get up and walk around. Again, by working with the feeling, you take away the appar-ent obstacle's power. This is true of all the *nivaranas*. These so-called obstacles are really unembodied parts of ourselves. The moment we move with these feelings rather than resist them, they evaporate.

Even the voice of doubt that says, "This is a waste of time. I'm not doing anything. I'm not getting any-where!" can be overcome in this manner. Even that voice evaporates when we pay attention to it and en-gage with it, not as a debating partner, but simply as part of our experience. This voice arises from internal concern. We are so used to operating from a map, one that we ourselves have constructed, that we find it very challenging to be without one, even for short periods.

In turning to an internally generated meditation object, we now move to a different modality and examine sensa-tions at the gate of thoughts and emotion. This mind gate is normally associated with what we call thoughts, essen-tially little bits of narration, stories composed of words and sometimes images, like short clips from a movie. We often find ourselves daydreaming as if these short clips were playing inside us. The capacity that we call imag-ination is a very powerful meditation object. If we can learn to approach the mind gate and use it as an object of meditation, we can maximize the impact we have.

The difference between the mind gate and the other sense gates is that its objects are self-generated. We are so used to seeing ourselves as observers of events that "happen" to us that we are unaccustomed to directly intervening in our own inner experience in this manner. If we develop this capacity, it becomes a powerful tool in our growing collection of meditation approaches. Normally, if a sensation arises, a thought immediately arises at our mind gate telling us what the sensation "means." We will be dealing with this feature later in our explorations; right now it is enough to recognize the ubiquity of what we call thoughts, the events at the mind gate that arise in this manner. This is why the act of choosing a mental object to concentrate on is so powerful.

EXERCISE
White Ball Breathing

This week's simple meditation exercise uses the mind gate. With eyes open or closed, all we do is visualize on the tip of our nose a radiant, shining little ball — like a ping-pong ball, or a white pebble, or a white pill. Whatever image comes is fine, as long as it is radiant. The color white is even optional initially — it could be green or blue or whatever, as long as it is glowing, bright, radiant. This gives us tremendous freedom to be flexible in our approach. As we breathe out, we imagine that it smoothly glides away from us, and as we breathe in, it comes back. We are not concentrating on the sensation of the breath in this exercise. Rather, we are using the breath as a metronomic device to help us watch this imagined white ball as it moves to and from the tip of our nose. Our breathing is merely a timing device, so as we breathe out, the ball goes away from us, but we are still present with it as it moves. And as we breathe in, it comes back and we are still present with it. We never lose contact with it. But if we do lose contact with it — for example, if one of the *nivaranas* takes over for a moment — it is the same old story: we relax, come back to the exercise, and start again.

The mind, being a bit of a monkey, is bound to play around with this exercise for a while. It'll give us a pink rock, or a white bunny rabbit, or some other thing. That's when we do the judo technique. Whatever we get, we work with that. We don't argue. And if we don't argue, but stay with our intention to visualize a small, radiant white ball, very soon we'll get the white ball. Initially perhaps we will imagine other things, but as in our other experiences of *shamata*, as we calmly persist, the white ball comes in the end.

Of course, the same thing will happen as with previous objects. We'll get fantasies and irritations — agitation, dullness, attraction, aversion, and doubt; all these things will manifest. Interestingly, dullness is one of the *nivaranas* the white ball deals with particularly well because the mind finds the radiance of the ball interesting, at least initially. Make the ball as bright and radiant as you can, and it becomes an absorbing mental object.

You're probably saying, "I can't see the ball!" That's because it's an object of imagination. It doesn't have to look like a physical ball. It's the thought of a ball. Sometimes it will appear like a white ball. Other times it might be the sensation of a white ball. It can be anything. Mental objects have no form. They merely clothe themselves with associations.

Overcoming Obstacles

This week we take an important step: making a self-generated object the focus of our meditation, rather than using inputs from one of our sense gates. All the same features apply. We pay attention to it with effort (*vitaka*) and savor its expression (*vicara*) while following it as it moves away from and toward our nose as we breathe in and out. Expect the obstacles (*nivaranas*) to manifest, particularly dull sleepiness. The brighter the little white ball can be, the more dullness can be overcome. Be like a judo player, though: don't fight with obstacles — roll over in front of them! Very soon the obstacles will lose their power, and the shining white ball will move serenely for our three minutes.

Questions and Comments

That was very difficult. It took me more than three minutes per day.

Don't work too hard! Meditation should be really easy.

Although I was trying to see a white ball, eventually I gave up and tried to imagine the sensation of a ball but without the image of the ball. Is that OK?

You are raising some important points. Instead of a white ball your image can be literally anything from your imagination. It's a mental object, so its form is not important; it might be a feeling, as you indicate. Sometimes we get caught up in trying to visualize exactly what we think the object should be. All that thinking and "*should*-ing" is unhelpful. We can end up creating obstacles for ourselves by setting artificial expectations that we cannot meet. It's very important that meditation is easy. If it's not easy, it cannot be transformative. Indeed, our *effort* is the part of ourselves that we wish to understand. But if we persist for long enough, we will succeed without effort.

In traditional writings on meditation, this effortlessness is sometimes called "the way of *sugata*." *Sugata* refers to ease and bliss; and becoming effortless and blissful, with flexibility and ease of being, is a fruit of *shamata*. In Western culture, being persistent sometimes has the connotation of gritting our teeth, as if we were doing a workout. But the idea here is not to break into a sweat to get the job done. There is a significant difference in meaning between *persistence* and *effort*. We think, "no pain, no gain," but trying to meditate like that is a wrong approach. It is more like developing a habit. We need to be persistent in order to develop a different way of being, even if it is just for three minutes a day.

Our persistence should be like the persistence of water. An old proverb sums up this attitude well: "Water cuts through stone, not by cutting hard, but by cutting often." We need to be like water — effortless but persistent. Meditation practice is like filling a lake with raindrops. You can hardly see it fill, but over time you'll have an expanse of water. On the other hand, if we make our practice an exercise of effort without the ease and flexibility of *vicara*, we will utilize our goal-oriented mapmaker: we will be within the thought of effort rather than in the continuity of meditation. The moment we get off the meditation cushion, our meditation is gone. If you have a glass of cloudy water, all you have to do is set it on a table and walk away. It will settle on its own.

Our task is to pick up a collection of tricks, useful techniques. There is not anything particularly special about any of them. Indeed, the best way to deal with meditation advice is to treat it with interest rather than duty. It's as if you were walking up a mountain and someone said, "Around the corner is a nice view." As you round the corner you will probably look, but there is no obligation to look. You are easy with it. No one said, "You must look!" Meditation techniques are exactly like that advice. They are not in any way saying, "You must!" *Must* is the language of effort. It's best to abandon all those injunctions and replace them with persistence. When effort is abandoned, insight arises. If you over-tighten the strings of an instrument, you will be unable to play in tune. Settle effortlessly into playing the notes so that the music can come out.

Two further ideas are helpful in dealing with thoughts coming in and disturbing our attempts to follow the white ball. First, thoughts are associated with tension. All we have to do is relax, and the thought goes away. So when a thought comes, don't immediately go back to the white ball by using effort. I suggest that you go with the thought. Let the thought have its day! Then, with an attitude of gentle persistence, go back to the white ball. Often the thought is associated with a sensation in our body. We let something go, relax a muscle, and the thought stops. Stresses trigger reactivity. So don't ignore the thought or think, "I'm going to put this away and go back to the white ball," because the white ball then becomes a thought itself.

Second, thoughts are not bad. They are manifestations of the incredible sensitivity of mind. We're not wanting to dominate the mind, to make it do all this stuff as if by force. We want to dance with our mind, like a gentle partner. This is a helpful way to work with arising thoughts. Eventually they will be of great interest. What we are doing now is befriending them — as if they are birds at our bird feeder. Right now they are still a bit wild perhaps, but eventually they'll land on our outstretched hands, even though they come from the outside. We're learning to be relaxed and aware. This is *sugata*.

Should our eyes be open or closed?

As I mentioned earlier, it doesn't matter here, not at all. The attraction of closing one's eyes is to shut down the vision gate, as it is such a powerful mode of sensation. The problem is that it is very easy to go into dream states with the eyes closed. This is why some people find it better to meditate with the eyes open. It's quite possible to have your eyes open and not be endlessly distracted by what you see.

All I see is a white blur.

A white blur is fine initially. Just make sure it shines. *Vitaka*, remember, is concentrating on an object. *Vicara* is going along with the object. In this case, the object, the shining white ball or the white blur, is moving, so we are developing *vicara* because we're following the moving object. Our concentration doesn't waver, but it is now able to track along with this moving object. You can easily do this with your eyes open. But if something catches your eye and takes you away, come back to the object of concentration. Having a light touch is very important in an exercise like this.

Are we holding the ball somehow?

Not really — it's floating on the tip of our nose! We visualize a ball about the size of a ping-pong ball, white and glowing like a 15-watt light bulb. Despite all these instructions, it is almost certainly going to be difficult to visualize that! You'll probably find that your mind will produce something else for you. Don't worry.

Unfortunately, that's the way our mental faculty works. It's so creative that when we give it an instruction, until it's calmed down and realizes what we are up to, it tends to give us something else. But if we can visualize a white ball, that's great. And if not, it will come after a while.

I am feeling challenged by this exercise because when I closed my eyes, I was expecting to somehow independently see a white ball. And what I ended up seeing was a kind of a mental construct, coming out of the depths of my mind. It wasn't in my vision, but I could mentally visualize it.

That is the white ball, of course, for the construct is merely the intention. Intend for it to be glowing and shining, and you will eventually get yourself a tiny glowing, shining white ball. Your intention is your object of concentration. But our minds don't like being told what to do. So part of the faculty we're developing is the ability to make our minds flexible, tamed, responsive to our requests. The important element of this meditation is simply the intention.

So whether you get a white ball or not, it doesn't matter as long as your intention to have a white ball is there. And whatever that intention manifests as, even if it's a pink bunny rabbit, that'll be fine. This intention manifests as whatever your mental equipment decides to give you. Have the intention of a white ball, and eventually that will come too. You don't have to worry too much.

Only read on once you have done
your seven days!

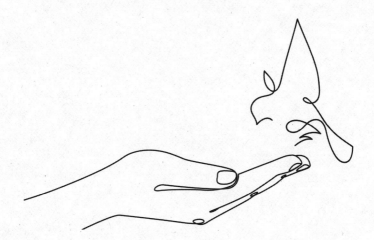

CHAPTER FIVE

Working with the Map

We've been gradually progressing in our choice of meditation object, what we decide to pay attention to. Having started with external objects such as a candle or bell, we moved last week to an internally generated object, a white ball.

This progression has a method to it: to gradually move our focus to the signs, the images and words, the names and memories that compose our internal model of the world, rather than sensations themselves. This is to move from phenomena arising at one of the five sense gates, which are our normal foci of meditation, to the sixth gate, that of the mind itself. By choosing to work with the sixth gate, with thoughts and ideas, we are beginning to develop the capacity to see the signs, those images and words, themselves. Normally we react to the signs, either by action or by following all the associations they trigger, by thinking about what they "mean." By deliberately choosing as the object of our meditation something that exists only in our imagination, we are developing our capacity to observe the signs themselves rather than merely reacting to them. This is a really important development in our exploration of meditation.

We normally adopt the comfortable idea that there is an external world that is being transmitted to us through our sense gates in some direct manner. After all, we navigate around our environment, interact with one another, and consume opinions and news about our shared world without much difficulty. But it only takes a moment's reflection to realize that our experience of the "external" world is mediated through our senses and it is our senses that actually provide inputs to us. Normally, we don't experience these inputs and the signs generated from them before reacting to them. So, for example, when something happens and we say it is nice or nasty, or good or bad, that reaction we have is not in fact the first cognitive event. The event happened before we passed judgment in that way. Indeed, in describing the process of cognition, our everyday language uses a very interesting term: we say, "I *recognize* that!" The *re-* prefix on the word *cognition* that creates the word *recognition* is an indication that the process is reflexive; that's to say, in recognition, cognition has been repeated. The cognized has been cognized again — it has been re-cognized.

So what is this repeated cognition of cognition? By what rules does it operate? When we say that we recognize something, we are indicating that it has a name, an identity that we have affixed to it. Recognition is the process that ascribes names and identities to whatever arises at our gates of experience. Those names and identities are not present in the initial phenomena themselves. They are added to those inputs in a process that all of us have spent many years developing — from our first attempts at naming things in early childhood, to the influences we have received from our parents, background, and education, to the experiences we ourselves have internalized and learned in forming our character. Indeed, until something is recognized, it cannot be nice or nasty, or good or bad. All those labels and characteristics arise from recognition. The problem for most of us is that this process of recognition is not part of our conscious awareness. By the time we are aware of what is happening, we've already reacted to the signs that arose from this process of double cognition, and so we end up preconditioned to act in a particular way, based on our preconceptions and memories rather than on the basis of the arising phenomena themselves.

A further element can be added to this important insight. Cognitive psychology has now confirmed what was known by meditation traditions for millennia, namely that our reactions to things are mainly learned. Even disgust, which would appear to be completely innate, is actually learned. For example, in Asian

countries such as Thailand and Vietnam, people eat insects. To most Westerners such a habit seems instinc-
tively repulsive. But if you actually learn to do it from
a young age, it's not disgusting. Perhaps an even more
graphic example is that young children don't find their
excrement disgusting. Any parent will confirm that
young children will happily play with their own feces.

The realization that a major part of what we recognize is
learned highlights the process of recognition as something intensely interesting and important. It is clear
that this is a substantial element of how we construct
our experience of the world. This has direct relevance
to meditation. Our initial task is to calm the mind, and
while the possession of a calm mind brings an obvious benefit in and of itself, it also allows this second
capacity, that of becoming aware of percepts — those
first movements of mind that occur before recognition
takes place — so that recognition itself can be seen. If
we are ever going to get control of our lives and not be
so reactive and disturbed by events, we need to have
knowledge of this process of recognition. Otherwise,
our prejudices, our likes and dislikes, are going to color
our experience in an uncontrolled manner. We will always have the feeling that we're out of control, that we
are being buffeted about by things we can't get a handle
on. In short, we will never attain *vipassana*, clear seeing, and discover the base of unclouded awareness that
was there all along.

There is a famous saying: "If stones hurt your feet, there are two things you can do. You can cover the world with leather, or you can cover your feet with leather." Often we try to cover the world with leather by creating a perfect life — living in gated communities, having perfect jobs and smooth relationships where nothing disturbs us. As events change, however, the high maintenance and inevitable failure of this approach gradually overcome our efforts. It would be far more effective to cover our feet with leather. Then when things happened that could disturb us, we would have a choice as to how to respond rather than reacting reflexively. Indeed, we could say that we learned how to respond rather than react. With this precious knowledge we can overcome the predicament of being a victim of external events, a victim of our own unconscious and reflexive reactivity that requires us to act automatically in ways governed more by our past experience than by what is actually happening.

One sees this capacity in martial arts movies. The hero, normally some sort of monk in layperson's clothes, even if attacked, doesn't see the assailant as attacking them. They don't cringe. They are not reacting to what the attack "means" — they are responding to the actual event. They move to embrace arising circumstances rather than reflexively attempting to avoid them. They have covered their feet with leather and so can respond rather than react to what is happening to them.

EXERCISE
Traveling over the Map

Here is an addition to the moving white ball meditation that makes the exercise much more engaging. As the shining white ball leaves on each outbreath, have it go progressively farther and farther, and then return on each inbreath. Mark its progress.

Have it go an arm's length and back for a few breaths, then out to the walls of the room you are in and back, then to the walls of your house and back, then to the center of your town and back. Then have it travel to the capital city of your state or country, then to the edge of your continent, then over the sea to the edge of the next continent, then on, traveling away from the planet into the atmosphere, then to the moon, on and on with each expanding journey, traveling straight like an arrow, leaving from the tip of your nose on the outbreath and returning back there on the inbreath. Continue outward and farther, to the nearest planet and back, then to the sun and back, then the next nearest star, then the center of the Milky Way, then out to the next galaxy, and then on out to the edge of the universe, returning back on the inbreath. Eventually the white ball goes so far, it goes to infinite space. You can follow this as a progression, using the faculty of *vicara*, the ability to stay engaged with this moving object as it flies farther and farther. Allow your imagination to engage with this blissful experience, traveling with the shining white ball, calm and clear in your mental space.

You can also allow it to come back in stages, traveling shorter and shorter distances with each breath, until it's finally not moving at all, merely sitting on your nose and glowing as the breath goes in and out.

This exercise allows us to use our world map along with the white ball. It's an expression of creativity. It becomes interesting as we play with our imagination, all the while following the ball closely, since our concentration never leaves its object. It might take three minutes or a little longer, but there is no need to get to infinite space as if it is a destination. Traveling in the world map is enough. Indeed, once we engage with this we don't really have to think of how long we have been doing it, as if traveling with the ball is some task we have to carry out. *Vicara* doesn't mind. Distance and duration have been transcended. Effortless concentration can stay with the journey wherever it goes. There is no physical obstacle. We're allowing our mental apparatus to move smoothly.

Bringing the Map into Focus

Having chosen a mental object for our meditation, now we begin an exploration of how we create our mental space. It is interesting to watch our mentally generated white ball travel over our mental map of the space in which we live — from the limits of our body, to the limits of the house, the town, the country, the planet, right out to the limits of the cosmos itself. Our world is actually a map, and working with it deliberately in our short meditation periods brings this construct into focus. Of course, we are developing our *vitaka* and *vicara*, and our *nivaranas* will still manifest as before, but hopefully they will begin to weaken. Alongside this we are doing something else as well: we are bringing into our awareness how we make the world in which we spend our lives.

Questions and Comments

With the white ball I have been going to the outer planets. Is it OK to stay there for a few breaths, or do I need to come back on every inhale?

I think it's best to come back every time, because this is not meant to be an exploration of space. It's more of an exercise in mental flexibility. One could say that *shamata* is like making dough. You have to knead the dough to make it pliable, pull it and stretch it this way and that. Here we go beyond the limits we set on ourselves based on the map we have of our experience. So certain things seem possible, and certain things not possible. The idea of *shamata* is to go beyond what's reasonable. It's not reasonable to go out to Alpha Centauri in a single breath, but it's not impossible. By using our imagination, we're looking to generate that level of flexibility.

Now that I've been at it for a few weeks, I find these three-minute practices more helpful than trying to sit for long periods.

I agree. Short and focused can be preferable to heroic exercises done for hours and hours, particularly for beginners. Meditating for long periods can sometimes lead to trance states, where we are more or less sleeping on our cushion.

When I do this exercise, I experience going toward the vastness, but then I can't find a center.

We are not trying to find a center here. We are not trying to travel from an established "here" to an established "there." Our rational mind, our mapmaker wants to make a map of our experience. It's a fundamental function of mind. When you do an exercise like this, a part of you wants to understand it, make sense of it. It is almost as if we want to make a map of the map! Our job is to create short exercises that go beyond the map, to enter the impossible, the unreasonable, using the very faculty of mind that creates our sense of the reasonable and possible. It's like we are trying to escape an overprotective auntie who wants to run our life for us in terms of gain and loss, fame and obscurity, success and failure, praise and blame. Meditation gives us the chance to dance freely without these judgments. But most of us never escape the map. We've always got some model of what we're doing. Some books lay out meditation like it is a physical journey, one step to the next, all the way to some destination called "enlightenment." Our task is a little different. It is to develop the ability to see this story, this wish for a destination that we unconsciously map for ourselves. By seeing this, ultimately we learn from ourselves, rather than from a map of ourselves.

I find as I do this exercise I get very disturbed by thought.

Thoughts are associated with tension. All we have to do is relax something, and the thought goes away. It's like the famous "three R's" we adopt when confronting a problem: *relax*, *release*, and *return*. When a thought comes, don't immediately go back to the white ball by using effort. That creates the tension that triggers thought. Then you have to suppress the thought, which is another thought.

Rather than struggle this way, I suggest that you go with the thought. *Relax* — let the thought have its day. *Release* your agitation. Then, with the attitude of gentle persistence, *return*. Go back to the white ball and start again.

Only read on once you have done
your seven days!

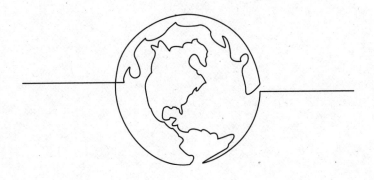

CHAPTER SIX

Never Leaving Our Own Bed

Asian meditative traditions often imply that the center of our being is located in the heart, not the head. This comes as a surprise to some of us, who have been fed a steady diet of science fiction stories in which the brain is depicted as a computer that can somehow be separated from the body and uploaded into a new container. We see the brain as the control system where everything happens and the body as a support system — a kind of appendage. As with a stick figure, the body just supports the head.

But as we begin to meditate, we realize that the actual place from which our experience is emerging is not the head. Indeed, as we start to become free of our reflexive mapping of experience, the head begins to feel more like an element of something much vaster and more encompassing. Sometimes in the Thai tradition they refer to the "heart mind," reflecting this shift in our center of being. This is not a reference to the physical heart. It's a reference to the center of gravity of the body, somewhere in the center of the chest, a little below the arms.

This feeling of a shift in the center of our being is subtle but pervasive. As we begin to see our experience as a display, it is as if we ourselves are embedded within it. Even though we appear to be continually busy, preoccupied with events happening in a world outside us, this is not really the case. As we relax our reactivity, we increasingly realize that we are profoundly connected to events that we have previously regarded as external to us — as the "real" world out there. We recognize that all of our experience, everything that occurs to us, arises through the six gates — the five gates of sensation and the sixth of the mind. This realization does not separate us from everything we see and experience, as if we are some kind of observer. Rather, it enables us to recognize that our inner state and the outer world are deeply connected. Like the body and brain become reconfigured in the heart mind, the outer and inner world become reconfigured in a greater unity.

It takes time for this to sink in. We are so used to reacting to "external" events that we have to take time to stop. The term *external*, or any reference to the "real" world, is an inference, a supposition, an idea developed from our actual experience, which must always be our sensations and cognitive impressions themselves. But as we become more conscious of these impressions, a transformation begins to happen. Synchronicities emerge in unexpected ways. It starts with having time to stop and smell the roses. But as it deepens, our preconception of being a self in a world begins to reconfigure, and a greater unity manifests.

Because this greater unity always contains inner and outer elements together, it is often described as unchanging. The Tibetan Buddhist tradition says we "never leave our own bed." Instead of seeing ourselves as isolated beings, navigating an external world by means of maps based on our experience and memory, this deeper engagement unifies both map and mapmaker in a greater whole. As we become more relaxed in the face of arising experience, the narrative that places "me" in the center of a storyline begins to dissolve. We see alternatives that were perhaps not so obvious before. Our sense of fitting in to some established position in the world, or living in a routine, doing what we always do, begins to expand into a more fluid expression. This new understanding is not to say that experiences do not happen, or that we are somehow isolated from them as a kind of watcher. Rather, it is to begin to see ourselves as paired with our environment and to increasingly be able to respond to events in an authentic manner.

Our dreams offer a classic illustration of the permeability of what we consider the "real world" or the "external world." Although for many of us dreams fade fast when we awaken from sleep, all of us have experienced dreams as being very real, as real as our waking experience. Indeed, nightmares can be so scary that many children are afraid of going to sleep. There is a famous story about this. A poor man goes to sleep, and in his dreams, he wins the lottery. Suddenly he is lifted out of poverty into a world of glamour and riches. He buys a huge house and a sports car. He dates beautiful women and before long settles down and starts a family. He begins to make investments, building a business empire to expand his winnings. Things go well for some years, but eventually he gets greedy and makes some bad decisions. In the end he loses everything. His house is foreclosed, his cars are repossessed, and his wife leaves him. He ends up living on the street, a poor man again. Then he wakes up.

Did any of these events happen to him? He awoke where he went to sleep, and even if he remembered the entire story of his dream, he never left his own bed throughout the whole of it. This is a fruitful question to ponder. Although we might say that none of the dream events happened in the real world, it is worth considering this question. The real world also arises through the same six gates, like his dream did. It is this arising we wish to understand better.

We are now more than a month into our meditation practice, and we have worked to develop a capacity to hold attention on a chosen object. Over the past two weeks that object has been entirely internal, a shining ball, moving back and forth from the tip of our nose, in a typical head-centered way. It is not an externally received object, such as the candle flame or the sensation of the breath.

Now is the time to engage more deeply with our experience of that imaginary object. Rather than imagining the white ball as moving back and forth over our world map, traveling farther and farther out into the galaxy, we can reconfigure this practice so we remain unmoving throughout the course of it, never leaving our own bed. To do this, we will imagine a white bubble growing larger and smaller from our center as we breathe, rather than a ball moving away from and back toward us.

EXERCISE
White Bubble

In this exercise, you imagine yourself being enveloped in a bubble. Initially imagine a bubble centered in the middle of your chest. It is white, glowing; not very bright but a soft white like a low-wattage light bulb. The bubble starts small, and as you breathe in it gets a little bigger, and then as you breathe out it shrinks back to its original size. As you breathe in a second time, it grows and envelops you on all sides, and as you breathe out it shrinks back into a small bubble in your center.

Imagine the bubble growing in size with each breath, reaching to the walls of your room and then back, then to the edge of your house and back, as you breathe in and out. Take whatever number of breaths you like between size increases. It can get bigger and bigger, expanding to the edge of your yard, to the center of your town or village, to the capital city of your country or state, and so on, each time shrinking back to your chest on the exhale. Eventually it encompasses the entire universe.

If you have time, after it encompasses the universe, then have it shrink back down again sequentially, extending slightly less on each breath, until finally it is resting as a white bubble in your chest with every breath. Then rest there, the bubble glowing slightly more brightly on the inbreaths but not otherwise changing size.

See if you can sense the calmness that is manifested as you visualize the white bubble throughout this exercise. The calmness is not moving. See if in the center of that softly shining bubble you can locate that sense of calm. What we're doing as meditators is choosing an object to concentrate on, deliberately but without too much effort. It is more like we are allowing it to happen. We're very gently shepherding something.

Rediscovering Our Center

Shamata is like kneading dough; we do various exercises with clear intent, and gradually our capacity to direct our concentration and savor what we find grows more and more powerful and flexible, like dough that is becoming soft and smooth as we allow it to rise and fall. That is the effect of any repeated practice, even short ones like those we do here. But there is a second theme to our efforts. We are gradually settling our concentration in the center of our manifestation — the origin point from which all our mapmaking must necessarily begin. It is interesting to watch small children in this regard — they are so effortlessly centered in their own bodies. But as we grow up many of us lose our center, until in the end we can carry deep physical discomfort or even disease without noticing it. Now, as we enter our sixth week, we are beginning to bring it back home.

Questions and Comments

I find that when I look at the white bubble and try to focus, it changes on me!

Don't resist, because reactivity is all about resistance. Accept what you get, thinking, "That's fine. I'll use that." What will happen is your resistance will lessen because you're not actually fighting. The problem is that you're trying to follow a meditation instruction. In following instructions we judge whether we're doing it right or wrong, well or badly. That's where the problem lies with all meditation instructions: they have a tendency to self-defeat. The idea is to go beyond recognition, which means, of course, that there can't be a right or wrong way of doing it. So don't worry — whatever your mind gives you, respond with, "Fine, that's great. I'll work with that!" You will find very soon your mind will stop playing around and give you what you want.

The Tibetans have a wonderful metaphor: that the mind is like a monkey sitting in a tree surrounded by lots of fruits it can grab for. Of course, it'll give you anything but what you ask for — monkey style! But when you don't care, then the monkey gets bored and gives you what you want. Do your three minutes a day, and don't make a big deal out of it — make it as routine as possible. You'll find that the monkey will give up playing around with you because you're not reacting.

It was easy for me to get the hang of it initially, but then I got distracted.

Distractions are always going to happen. Be patient and don't react to them. It's not helpful to enter dialogues like, "I can't do this. I have to try harder!" Don't do any of that stuff because it's a trap that makes meditation more difficult — as if it's a task we have to do.

Thank you for these helpful instructions! I have found this white bubble exercise much easier to do than the white ball, and I had the experience of the middle of my chest as the center of my being, with the bubble located there. That was great. When that happened, I dropped right into it.

As I mentioned, a lot of meditators say that the center of our awareness is in the heart, and that's not the physical heart but the center of the chest. Some ancient cultures had similar views. The Greeks, for example, thought that the function of the brain was to cool the body, again because they held that the seat of awareness was in the center, not in the head. But in any event, I'm glad you had that experience. That's great.

What we experience as we do a meditation like this, even for three minutes, is the ornaments of the calm state. Now, the calm state can manifest as joy or happiness, or as clarity, or in many other ways. The calm state is the state of resting just as we are. And, of course, since each one of us is individual, and we change day to day, the calm state will have different ornamentations; it will feel different depending on our body makeup. But no matter how it manifests, the calm state itself always has the continuity of *vicara*. So although it may be calm joy, or it may be calm happiness, or it may be calm lightness, or it may be calm spaciousness or calm whatever, it's got that feeling of calm continuity. The key is to focus on that. It might be joyous one day and spacious another, or happy one day and sad another, but really it doesn't matter what quality it evokes. In the center of it, there's always going to be that continuity, that flow.

That calm center is a very valuable meditation object. One could say whatever we experience is an expression that arises out of this sense of calmness, but we lose contact with it. We get so energized by the qualities that emerge from our initial contact with our sense gates that we lose contact with arising sensation and enter a re-cognitive maze, with all the associations and meanings it contains. When this happens, as we make a world, we lose contact with ourselves.

Only read on once you have done
your seven days!

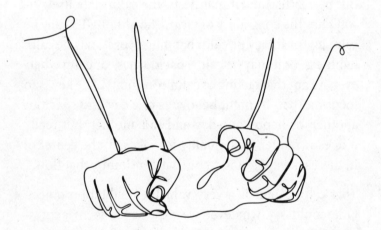

CHAPTER SEVEN

Bringing It to the Center

We've been developing a *shamata* practice, and last week we were developing a state of calm during meditation. Something quite magical manifests in that state of calm.

In the early 1970s one could travel overland to India from Europe, traveling across the Bosporus and on through Turkey, Iran, and Afghanistan. This was before the long series of invasions and the endless troubles, when Kandahar, the desert capital of southern Afghanistan, was still intact. It had a single paved road on the edge of it, and the rest of the city was a maze of narrow streets with no room for cars, edged on either side by flat-roofed adobe houses, with the famous Blue Mosque in the center. There was a small hotel made of concrete on that road, overlooking the old town; from there one had a great view over the sand-colored houses to the blue dome shimmering in the distance.

One evening the great orb of the sun was going down, and it was very quiet. All one could hear were animals calling — dogs barking and donkeys braying — set against the gentle rustle and bustle of the end of a hot day. As the sun faded from yellow to orange, the temperature cooled and a small breeze sprang up. Then someone began to play a flute.

It must have been a small metal flute, the inexpensive kind sold in the local market. It played small refrains, broken by periods of silence. But it was as if the flautist was playing that flute to the town itself. It was the most exquisite experience. A refrain sang out, and then a disparate sound would happen — perhaps a dog barking or someone calling. Then the flautist would play another refrain, and another sound would happen. Sometimes there was silence, and then the flute would play again. It was like a duet — the flute and the town, all enveloped as one in the steady silence of the setting sun. Stillness, then movement in that stillness; spontaneous. Then a response, a seemingly unconnected sound — perhaps a door slamming or a voice calling — that made the invitation for another short burst of music. Then silence again.

Because of the flute, the silence was never empty. The music and the silence and the sounds were one; whole. That's how direct experience manifests. All phenomena are in harmony, because one emerges from the other. For once, there was no reliance on a map, on an idea of what was happening. The flute had opened a door to just be there.

Normally we live our lives like navigators, like pilots relying on instruments to fly. But the flute made an invitation: come live on the inside, in harmony, rather than trying to make sense of it from a distance! As long as we are outside, relying on our controls, we always run the risk of becoming out of harmony with events as they are. We become turbulent, stirred up, disconnected.

As we learn how to be free to choose our own way, we gain the freedom to leave our model of how things are. In our normal way of learning we rely on a map, a structure that contains all our expectations and preconceptions, based perhaps on something we were told by someone else or an outcome from some event that happened to us in the past. All these elements get stored in our cognitive map, as modifications or improvements. The map gets denser and denser, more and more detailed. And then we live by it, guided continually, relying on it as our first response to every rising impression.

Meditation is all about getting free of this structure — not to destroy it, but to reconfigure our relationship to it. As with any powerful capacity, we need to practice taking command of the mapmaker, learning how to use it rather than having it use us. It is about being decisive, but in a strange and unusual way. For example, when we read the biographies of so-called spiritual masters, we often find that they do things for very practical reasons. They are not beyond learning. Many of them need to acquire new skills and abilities, and when they do, they simply get and perfect them. And then they go on to the next thing. We always think they are special, gifted in some magical manner, but when we understand them in this way we see that they are people who took control of their experience rather than being limited by their own conceptions about it. We could even say that the moment we take control of our own experience, we are already a master. We are a master of our own experience, even if only for that moment. This is an important recognition, something to take note of. Students don't do anything. All students do is accumulate. It's only when we start to apply what we have accumulated that we take ownership, and it's only through taking charge in that way that any deep change is possible. That is what mastery is all about.

A second point emerges here: The calmness we seek is not a state of abiding; rather, it is a state of clarity. The calmness we seek brings clarity to all experience. It is not an abiding and observing of experience. This calm is what allows us to access our experience before the mapmaking, reflexive mind makes sense of it. If we try to abide in calmness, to make calmness our home, we create a cut-off place from which we can observe and generate an internal commentary from within our map. But that is not what we're looking for. That calmness is conceptual. This is why *shamata* so often becomes a dead end. People use their *shamata* to abide. Even if that abiding is more and more continuous, it is essentially blind to direct experience itself.

We are looking to be like that flute player in Kandahar, responsive to events but not separated from them. We seek to be in a duet with our experience. In all the exercises where we are moving with an object, developing our capacity of *vicara*, we try not to merely abide while our object of concentration moves outside us. Our intention is to move with the object. If we merely abide while our object moves, we are in a little map, mapping "me" while the object moves outside us.

To find this state, we learn another way of being. It's not mystical, complicated, far away, or special. It's direct and unmapped. We will need to ease our way into it because it's a little unusual to be in experience and know it at the same time. The key is to follow the feelings we have. For some of us it might be warmth, or spaciousness, or quietude. Whatever manifests is a function of our own state. The important thing is to notice what joins all such sensations, to notice the current of calm that we begin to access in *vicara*, and now to make it a meditation object on its own.

EXERCISE
Rising and Falling Balls

This meditation exercise builds on our work with an internal meditation object. We can begin with the white bubble or the white ball, but once we are settled, we imagine two shining balls resting at our center. There is a white ball on top, small, like a shining point of light, and beneath it there is a red one, again shining and point-like. Two little points of light. Don't worry too much about the size of them. They have a bright, shining color and rest right in the middle of our body, in the center of our chest.

As we breathe in, we imagine the shining white ball rising up through our neck and into the center of our head. At the same time, the brilliant red ball travels down through our stomach and rests between our legs. Then as we breathe out, the red ball rises and the white ball falls, coming back to rest, one on the other, in the center of our torso. With every breath, we allow these balls to rise and fall. If we wish, we can have them travel farther and farther, but the important thing is that they travel within the core of our body, up and down, rather than in front of us, as we might normally be inclined to visualize them.

If we find the red and white balls too difficult, we can use two white balls, one rising and one falling, or two green or blue balls, or whatever. They can be French poodles; it doesn't matter! The main thing is that they are shining and they start from the center of the body and rise and fall through the midline of the torso. Whatever we are imagining, they are right in the middle of our body. They're not in front of us going up and down as if we could look at them. They're right in the middle.

As we breathe during our three minutes, the balls edge a little higher and a little lower, so that they eventually come out from the center of the head and between the legs with each breath, rising up and falling down. It does not matter how far they go, but they can go farther and farther if you like. The main thing is that they return to the center with each outbreath.

If you've only just gotten comfortable with the expanding white bubble, you can approach this new exercise by initially doing the white bubble for a few breaths. And if you find the expanding bubble hard, do the white ball leaving from the nose! And if you find that one too difficult, go with the feeling of breath on the tip of your nose; and if that is too hard, go back to the candle or the bell. The key here is that we are choosing to place our attention somewhere, and then we're relaxing and allowing the experience to manifest without doing anything else.

Getting Free of the Mapmaker

To our rational mapmaking mind, having a direct experience like this seems potentially dangerous. After all, the narrative structure in which we live is a predictive device that can protect us from unexpected outcomes. For example, I sometimes have breakfast with my daughter's pet bunny. He has a map. He is always looking around in a state of reactive alarm, thinking something might be wrong. After a while he overcomes it. I am gradually training the bunny to be comfortable in the world. We're like that too. We've always got a plan. We think, "I've got to learn this," or, "I've got to do that!" Meditation is a chance to overcome this re-activeness. It's a "not doing." If you don't have a map, you're not doing; you are not reacting to warning signs given to you from what you think you are doing. One could say that the whole idea of doer and doing is a map thing. And that is not what we are looking for.

This is the reason for short meditations. In such short periods we can get a glimpse of that calmness before the map takes over. But once our mapmaker has digested what we are up to it is as if the mapmaker says, "I know what this is. I can do this!" The moment that happens we have a problem. Then the mapmaker's got hold of our meditation and tries to tell us how to do it — providing a commentary about whether we are meditating well or not. But we are actually meditating well when we are engaged but don't know we're meditating well! When we know we are meditating well, we're in a map, within the idea of meditating well. This is sneaky and slippery. It's something we have to work with in cunning ways. With increasing experience we'll find our own ways to get free of the mapmaker, with little glimpses of freedom before it takes over and re-establishes control once again.

Questions and Comments

Why do we locate the white and red balls in the middle of our body rather than somewhere else?

This is because we're learning about our center. As I mentioned earlier, as we become familiar with brief periods of *vitaka* and *vicara*, we find ourselves accumulating a feeling that we are here, centered and stable. This meditation exercise is quite deliberately working from such a centered feeling, rather than focusing our attention outside. Remember, all reference to outside and inside is entirely inferential. So here, we choose an imaginary sense object of our own making and locate it in our chest, where we cannot see it. We're going to start bringing the attention in, which is really the same as saying that we are going to start allowing our attention to rest where it actually is.

So are you saying the balls are actually there in some sense?

That depends on what you mean by "there." We map our experience, and because we're unconscious of our mapping, we're deeply unable to control ourselves. If I suggest to you a new "there" to start from, I'm providing another map for you to be unconscious of! Rather than that, it is better to begin to work with our experience, so we can take control of it and then figure out what in it is mapping and what is not mapping. Just for three minutes a day!

Does meditating on the shining balls have anything to do with direct experience? Isn't it something we're making up?

If you directly experience the balls, you have direct experience. Everything we experience comes through our minds, so we could say it is all made up. There is no experience that is not mediated through the mind in one way or another. But we tend to conceptualize direct experiences as things. Once our experiences are identified as things, they accumulate associations — they become nice or nasty, good or bad. They are no longer direct experiences. This is the whole challenge of what we are doing. True direct experience is without a label, without an association that ties the experience to our past memories. This process of identification, of labeling, acts to cover the experience that is being labeled with an identity; we then "know" what it is, and it is no longer direct experience.

In doing this week's practice I found that the image in my mind of the red and white balls kept breaking up. It wasn't a continuous image of the balls moving. It was bits and pieces. I am experiencing these balls like a series of photo frames that aren't seamlessly put together.

This could be seen as good news. It might be that you are a deep meditator and you are seeing the arising of consciousness moment to moment. In deep concentration one can actually get to the point where consciousness flickers as awareness arises intermittently with its object. All the traditions report this phenomenon.

But it is more likely another explanation, namely that for beginners, the mentally created objects are intermittent because the faculty of concentration is immature, so it is very easy for the image to get broken up. People often get hung up on this because they feel like they are not doing anything valuable. However, if we do it repeatedly, we will find that the image becomes more stable.

Our normal efforts lead to the conceptual. When we try to do something, we make a model of it and work to perfect what we are doing, guided by that map. But meditation is not like this. It's about developing a faculty of mind, an awakened awareness that is not defined by the map of meaning we have constructed for ourselves. This is a very alien and strange activity. But once we become used to it, it leads to a massive discovery, a discovery that there is something other than a map that we can live by. We can go off and explore foreign places, but if we are still stuck in a map moment to moment we are not going very far at all; we're merely changing the scenery that generates the map. But if we leave the map, we can go into our living room and enter a different universe.

Only read on once you have done
your seven days!

CHAPTER EIGHT

The Power of the Smile

One of the themes we have been developing over the past seven weeks is an examination of "the world." We live in a model, a shorthand version. This is not to say there isn't something out there. It's to point out that we don't directly experience it. This model we have is full of known things, but those things have been created in a process that we are normally unconscious of. With relatively simple analysis of how reflexes work, we can estimate that it takes approximately four hundred milliseconds to generate this model in response to any given sensation, moment by moment. This is quite a significant amount of time. It's equivalent to how long it takes to snap the fingers once or twice. So whatever the world is — and of course, strictly speaking, that's unknowable — we are a finger snap behind it at all times.

Studies have shown that our physiology acts to disguise this lag in our cognitive process wherever it can.

Precise mechanisms operate to produce a delay so that when we start to move — say, to pick something up — the areas of the brain that initiate movement activate after the parts of the brain that are involved with the awareness of that movement. There is a small period of anticipation in all our actions. If this were not the case, if the delay were not compensated for in some way, we would always be behind our actions! All this data, both logical and scientific, points to the same conclusion: The present moment that we experience is not truly present. It is only present in the map of meaning we have created for ourselves.

The problem we suffer from is that the things in the world we have mapped are not merely named; they are also injunctions that have opinions and memories attached to them. When, say, I pick up a clock, I don't merely recognize this set of sensations, which I infer as being an object, as "a clock." I also have opinions. I might like it or not like it. Perhaps I remember it from yesterday or have an idea about changing the battery. There are little instructions attached to every item we identify. So this metaphor of a map is not fully accurate; it is not merely a piece of paper! Rather, this guide we generate moment to moment contains countless injunctions to act. "I like this one," "I must get that," "I've got to do this!" These little urgings are what make us so unsettled. You could say our maps are pushing us around.

The first goal of meditation is to become aware of this internal narrative, this guide by which we live. If we can't disconnect our reflexive reactivity from the map that provokes it, we will never, ever be able to get control of what happens to us. We might be able to create environments that suit us — like the gated communities mentioned earlier — but this is highly paranoid. We are endeavoring to control the map instead of controlling the mapmaker. Even if we do control the map, we always have in the background this feeling of being in danger, of there being things that threaten us.

So, once we have reached the point where we are developing a calm state, one of the purposes of such a state is to separate ourselves from our reflexive reliance on internal guides and maps. They will still be there; they are not going to disappear, because they are a fundamental element of our mental operations. But what we can do is disconnect our reflexive reactivity so they do not dominate our lives. And the more we develop *shamata*, the more that capacity can grow.

By developing in this way, we're exercising a faculty of mind that no one ever taught us. We were taught to be concentrated, but we were never taught to be calm. Yes, of course, an exasperated parent may have said, "Calm down, calm down!" But that is not the same thing at all. The ability to access map-free calmness is a unique capacity — and it is extremely valuable. It's a way of living that transforms everything because, as we develop a calm center, our reactivity ceases to be reflexive. At that point, we can choose whether to react or not; it is not just a knee jerk.

There's a trick to accessing this valuable state, and it arises from an interesting observation. Most of us have seen statues of the Buddha — those images of a meditating man that seem to be in many shops and restaurants nowadays. Perhaps you even own one. But if you look closely at them, you will see that the Buddha always has a slight smile. You are never going to find a seated Buddha with a frown on his face or anything like that; they always smile. Why does the Buddha smile? There's a real secret here. It is this: if you smile, it's easier to maintain the calm state. Again, we can refer to Pali terms, that ancient language the meditators used. *Sukha*, which is happiness, is a prerequisite for *samadhi*, which is a calm, serene, intuitive, and concentrated state. That's why the Buddha smiles.

Human beings are somewhat strange in this regard. If you make the facial features of a smile, the energy of a smile will manifest. So just by smiling, you will experience that feeling of warmth that a smile brings. It will permeate your body. The facial movement of smiling and the sensation of smiling are linked together. So all you have to do is smile. The warmth that the *sukha* feeling manifests makes the calm state more stable.

In our meditation, whenever we get distracted, what we normally do is make a critical comment — something like, "Oh, I got distracted. I have to return to my meditation object!" But that kind of reaction can be counterproductive, because it generates a state of tension, and consequently we then try to re-enter the calm state from a state of tension. Now we have a different path.

When we get distracted, we remember to smile. "Oh, I got distracted. Never mind, just smile. I'm happy to go back into the calm state again." This is a really valuable piece of advice: when you get distracted and you find that your calm state is unstable, instead of being frustrated, smile! If you maintain the smile as you re-enter the calm state, you'll find your entry into the calm state can become automatic. And you'll experience that precious effortlessness that has already been talked about.

EXERCISE
Sitting with a Smile

The way to approach this initially is to split our meditation into two parts. First, we work with the red and white balls, or the white bubble, or the single white ball, or the breath, or the bell sound, or the candle — whatever we feel comfortable with. Then we smile and allow the technique to fade into calmness without any object of meditation at all.

If we are using the red and white balls, one idea is to allow the white and red balls to rise and fall farther and farther, until eventually they go so far that they dissolve altogether. Then we sit, resting in that calm state, with a slight smile.

We rest our awareness on the warmth of that smile. As we do so, we relax more and more deeply into that warm and safe space.

Calm Clarity with Open Eyes

Once you've got the hang of this exercise, sometime during the course of your day, try simply looking at something and allowing calm clarity to be present. It is always there, but shiny things with all their associations and injunctions always cover it over. Just smile, and once you get a taste for it, you can have calm clarity in any experience.

When you are meditating, if you get distracted, smile. Go back and start by entering the calm state using the balls or the bubble or whatever. Or, if you can enter the calm state, just enter. It doesn't matter how you get there. And then if something is distracting you, allow it to distract you. Then smile and settle back.

Sit with that smile. It does not matter if your eyes are open or closed. In some respects, meditation with the senses open develops a stability you can take with you into everyday activity. So ultimately meditating with the eyes open is preferable, but if you find it too distracting, close your eyes. When you are used to it, you will be able to develop a calm state even though your eyes and senses are open and all kinds of inputs are coming in. Sometimes this is called non-meditation to make this point. The difference is not whether we are sitting on a cushion or not; it is, rather, whether we are completely in the *shamata* state. If we can attain that state, we're covering our feet with leather rather than trying to cover the world with leather. We can go anywhere.

Questions and Comments

Do I actually have to smile?

Yes, though it can be a subtle smile playing on your lips. When we smile, we tend to feel happy. The very act of smiling produces a sense of happiness. So do smile — don't think about smiling! Holding a slight smile helps in generating *sukha*, and *sukha* acts as the base, the foundation upon which our calm clarity can rest.

I feel I cannot get into the calm state and remain there to smile!

That is because it is the other way round. By smiling it is easier to access the calm state. One could say, however, that it is simple, but not easy. Obviously a not doing is as simple as you can get. But it's not easy because we are used to using effort in everything we do. If we use effort, we are "doing" meditation. By trying to do it, we create obstacles for ourselves. In this situation there are two ways we can respond: One is that we can fall back to things we are familiar with. So fall back to the white balls or the expanding bubble or the moving ball, or go back to the breath or an external object. All these techniques are a bit like a series of circles surrounding the open field of not doing. The second way is almost magical. Right in the middle of whatever activity we are undertaking, we can recover the very same calm clarity without an object; it's right there in the middle of it! It is accessible at all times. Rest there with a smile.

I find that I can get physically into a calm state, but my mind keeps racing.

Yes, it will. But then, just smile. We have spent our whole lives in reflexive reactivity, and not only in the daytime either. At night, we dream frenetically. Some people speak in their dreams; they toss and turn. It never stops! This is a habit that's very deeply ingrained. So developing calm is like stopping a speeding train: It's going to take a few miles of track. You can't stop it immediately. So, don't worry. Just smile.

Only read on once you have done
your seven days!

CHAPTER NINE

The Whole Body of the Breath

Through our series of sequential meditations over the past weeks we have gradually approached the experience of being calm without having an object or an experience to be calm about. Our awareness doesn't need an object. It can be aware of itself. It's self-aware. But this is not self-consciousness, as in shyness or social inhibition. It is being aware of calmness itself. Once we are aware of calmness itself in this way, we can turn back to our object of meditation, but now as a whole body.

This term *whole body* needs explanation. Let's take the taste of chocolate. If you meet somebody who hasn't eaten chocolate, you can't say, "Do you like chocolate?" They would respond, "What are you talking about?" There are no words you can use to describe chocolate to someone who has not tasted it. It is sweet, but not sugary. It melts in your mouth, but it is not butter. No matter how hard you try, there are no words to describe chocolate that can substitute for the experience of tasting it. For someone who has never tasted it, you have to give them a piece of chocolate.

This reference to the actual experience of something could be described as its "whole body." It's not only an idea or a name. We can try to think about it, of course, but that is just a thought. And even when we get an actual taste of something, the meaning maker, the narrative producer gets to work: "Oh, I know what that is!" Our mental faculty then tries to reproduce it for us through memory and expectation, and that in turn creates an obstacle, because we don't want the reproduction; we want the genuine article. So we begin to dance with our own cognitive process. This is very much part of meditation, and it's not that our cognitive process is an enemy; rather, it's more like an overzealous friend. It is sincerely trying to help us. So we have to be super polite and kind and persistently find ways to get around it.

So let us revisit one of the simplest meditations we've done, the breath-watching form of *shamata* from week 3. (It's often called *vipassana* meditation, but in our school of thought, we have not gotten to *vipassana* yet.) Now instead of only watching the sensation of the breath on the nose or in the torso, let us extend our engagement. In traditional texts this is called "watching the whole body of the breath." This can be taken to refer to the entirety of the experience of breathing, the entire cycle of the breath, rather than a little point on the nose or body. It means every sensation that happens in the body as we breathe in, every sensation that happens in the body as we breathe out — the whole body of the breath. This becomes the field of our *vicara*.

This practice is actually quite powerful, because it's taking the flexibility of *vicara*, our savoring of experience, and combining it with our calm non-doing. In such a way we can re-engage with experience. We are no longer abiding in calmness and doing nothing. We are actually re-engaging with our full manifestation, the whole body of the breath, with calm clarity that has no expectations. One could call it presence; in any case, it is where most of us go wrong. The moment we act, we leave the calm state and enter a map of what we are doing, full of expectations and injunctions. But once we have this capacity, there is no difference between meditating and not meditating. Our calm clarity is always present.

Furthermore, as we engage with our breathing, we realize that it is not some "thing" to look at. We *are* breathing. It's not separate from us. This is the root of the confusion we all suffer from. Our language creates the impression that there are two things when there is actually only one. For example, when we look at someone else, we don't see them and their experience as separate. We only see them. There are not two things there. In our confusion we think there are two things here, in us, as if our experience and our body were somehow separate. We have to remind ourselves through calm clarity that there is actually only one thing. There only ever was one thing. We are breathing, and we simply rest our attention on the body of the breath. As we breathe out, the attention is with it. As we breathe in, the attention is with it. Our breathing and our attention are together.

Any arising experience can be an object of calm clarity. That's a very creative idea. We suddenly realize that meditation, in terms of moving with arising experience, can happen anytime, anywhere, with any experience. The necessity of taking a specific meditation object becomes less and less important once we realize that we're surrounded by meditation objects all the time.

So try to experience the calm clarity of meditation with the sense gates open rather than closing them down to only one. If you get too distracted, by all means close down. But do so knowing why you are doing so, like closing your eyes, for example. You are simplifying your sense fields. There is no magical reason to close your eyes. For, once someone has become familiar with arising experience, you wouldn't be able to tell by looking at them whether they were meditating or not. A meditator like that is moving with their own experience. This will be an important foundation from which we can see our experience clearly.

EXERCISE
Following the Breath

We are going to follow the sensations of breathing. To be present in our calm clarity, we are going to direct our clarity to rest with the whole body of the breath. We don't "look" at our breathing — there simply is no obstruction; clarity is just clear. Clarity is an absence of obstruction. And in that state, our breath will come into our body as we breathe in, and then it will leave our body as we breathe out. We can be conscious of the little sensations that happen as it does so. That *vicara* of our own orderly process is a great experience to have, not only because it's interesting in its own right, but because it is the beginning of a great spaciousness in which experience happens within calmness itself.

Reinhabiting Experience

Resting with the whole body of the breath is an invitation to embodiment. We talk about "our" body, as if it is a thing in a world of things, but actually our embodiment *is* the world of things. There is nothing else in our experience. Inhabiting experience in this way is only possible when we have reduced our reactivity, because reactivity always causes us to create distance, to separate ourselves from what is happening. Reactivity disembodies us, as if we were an actor, somehow separated from what is happening. By watching the whole body of the breath we are training ourselves in *re-membering*, reinhabiting, using our most essential function, the breath itself. Rest with the breath for three minutes. If you can remember to do it at other times during the day, great!

Questions and Comments

When you recognize thoughts coming through your mind, do you use an active process such as concentrating on a thought and letting it go, or do you let it run its course?

Actually both of those alternatives are forms of doing. Rather than applying some sort of antidote, move with the thought and don't do anything. You'll find that thought will run out of steam. The idea is to allow the thought to manifest, and your calm clarity stays with it. You're merely there; after all, the thought is you too. And it comes to an end, and another one soon begins. If that is too nebulous you can simply drop back into watching the whole body of the breath.

These techniques are a bit like learning to ride a bike. We are developing a knack of not doing. Our normal way of being is predicated on a doer and a thing done. But the base of *shamata* we are developing is to go beyond doing. Doer and done are all part of a map we have by which we are trying to navigate the world. But the territory we are seeking to inhabit doesn't have a doer and a done. Only the map does. To overcome the doer and the done is to gradually achieve an introduction to direct experience itself, to engage in experience without a map, without saying, "I have to do this or that." Like riding a bike, we learn to do what appears to be impossible, which is to do one thing, not two. When we are stationary on a bike we are wobbling this way and that, compensating for falling to one side or the other. Yet when the bike gets moving, suddenly we go through a portal into a state where everything is stable, seemingly without any effort at all.

Is it possible to follow the breath and watch the thoughts at the same time? Say, by giving 30 percent of my attention to the thoughts and 70 percent to the breath?

Yes, perhaps. But doing this would be a bit like making a poppy cake rather than a brioche! It's just a different kind of bread. If you follow thoughts they go into quietude, then another thought starts up. The main thing is not to abide. So be aware of the possibility that your returning to the breath might be a form of abiding, creating a place from where you are watching your breath. You might have a "breath abiding" seat from which you are observing thoughts. But our calm clarity, our thinking, and our breathing are not separated like that; they are one.

I can follow the breath by watching it, and I can follow the breath by being it.

Exactly. I'm in agreement with you. Keep working in that mode. When you meditate like this you are returning to the experience of the breath itself and not to the breath as an object of experience.

I think you are saying that our thoughts and breath are both ourselves. That helps me to not resist and push the thought away. I was taught to watch it. It's part of me. Thoughts are just energy.

Yes, I agree. My only comment would be on the word *watch*. Watching implies a watcher and a watched.

Is there any special breathing we should do here?

You can breathe through the mouth or breathe through the nose. I prefer to breathe through mouth and nose together, but you don't have to. And smile with that subtle smile we talked about last week. This is quite the reverse from learning some specialized skill. We are discovering what we've already got.

Is it possible to be doing something active, like walking or hiking, while maintaining the calm state within you?

Yes, of course. Furthermore, athletes learn to remain calm even in the highest states of pressure. Great performers, like singers or actors, inhabit their art in a similar manner. This is a capacity we see in many activities without realizing that it is generally relevant to all aspects of our lives.

Only read on once you have done
your seven days!

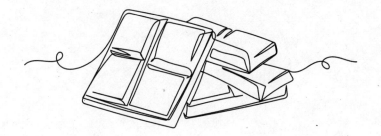

CHAPTER TEN

Controlling Thought

One of the most important features of meditation is thought. Thoughts come in two types: Some thoughts appear a little random initially, but as we get used to them, we see they are triggered by one sensation or another. Our mental apparatus takes in impressions, assesses them based on past experiences, and then provides feedback. But then we have the second type: proliferation. These are secondary thoughts that arise from associations set off by the first category of thoughts, which arise in response to events at the sense gates. One common form is the thought, "Yes, I have to do something about that!" For example, you may be sitting in meditation and suddenly feel a cold draft on your neck. That sensation may lead to a proliferation of thoughts, such as "I need to get a scarf so I won't be cold. I can't wait until summer! And I must do something about the draft. Maybe we should get the windows replaced. I wonder if the price will go down anytime soon…" Normally we are engulfed in an enormous amount of proliferated thought. This is what makes it so difficult for us to clarify our experience. Our experience is full of conditioned responses, which are proliferations and triggers for further proliferation. Not only is arising experience already multifaceted, but then it is multiplied one hundred times by associations.

As we meditate, thoughts become increasingly apparent. But thought in itself is not an enemy. Thought, in terms of our mental apparatus doing its business, is no more a foreign entity in our experience than breathing is, doing its business. It's merely another one of the gates doing its thing. There is no purpose in trying to stop thought any more than there is in trying to stop breathing.

If you leave thoughts to their own devices, they arise and fall away by themselves. They are of no tremendous importance. They are certainly not an enemy. It is proliferation triggered by arising thoughts that makes thoughts disturbing. This proliferation of thought is one of the major obstacles we come across in meditation. Proliferating thoughts take us away in various directions. After a little journey, we find ourselves coming back to what we were doing before the thoughts swept us off. Normally we are not aware of this, but the calm state is with us the whole time; we don't know it because we're always projecting away from it into our reactive conceptuality, which is the world of places to visit and jobs to do, and all the judgments of good and bad, failure and success, gain and loss that we find so exhausting in the first place.

All this noise, this proliferation of ideas, seems overwhelming, but always underneath it there is the calm state. So the calm state is absolutely not special. In fact it is totally ordinary. It is the most ordinary thing that we have. It's so ordinary, it's not an experience. This is a valuable insight. Important experiences stand out from the rest of our life; we say, "Oh, that was such an amazing time!" In some respects, people who try to abide in the calm state are trying to make the calm state such an experience — a place or location where something important will happen. It's a very attractive idea. However, the calm state has no characteristics at all. It rests with a smile. Its very ordinariness is its extraordinary power. Like air that surrounds everything, the calm state is totally pervasive. The calm state is present in all of our experience but because it's so ordinary, we totally miss it. We're looking for the extraordinary, the special event, the striking thing, and so we miss the calm state altogether.

So, in our journey over the past nine weeks, we have been gradually spiraling toward a recognition. It is this: This state that we are "developing" is actually already there! It's just that we spend our entire life leaving it. The non-doing that is the essence of a successful *shamata* exercise is present in the calm state in the first place. It is always there as a cognizant baseline, the ground zero of our cognitive process.

As a result, the calm state is totally reliable. Even if you could remove everything else, it would always be there. We can leave it, but it never leaves us. And so whenever are we getting freaked out or entranced or excited or into any other state, that state sits on top of this underlying state of calm, which is always present. And in many ways, meditation is this: the faculty of accessing that calm state. Not creating it; not generating it. One could say "discovering" it, but as we already have it, in many ways it's remembering, reconnecting, bringing something back that got covered over.

So how can we work with this insight? There are indeed simple techniques that allow us to gain mastery over thought. The technique for this week is one of them.

EXERCISE
Thinking Deliberately

One of the main features of meditation, even for short periods, is the arising of thoughts. Most people find this intensely irritating and want to stop thoughts altogether. But that intention is itself another thought! Like dealing with the *nivaranas*, those obstacles we considered in the early weeks of this journey, a better approach is to learn how to roll with thoughts, to go with them deliberately, for then we can achieve control over this feature of our experience that before felt absolutely beyond us.

The technique is simple. For this week's exercise, we spend a minute and a half deliberately thinking. Instead of being irritated by thoughts, we take ownership of them and think deliberately. We really work at thinking, initially by naming all that we are experiencing, and then by encouraging proliferative association based on those names. Suppose a mental picture pops into our head — first we name its contents, then we use our memory and appreciation to make a commentary about it. This can be done with inputs from any of the gates, including the mind gate itself. Just think deliberately, discursively, with real intensity.

To begin, set a timer for ninety seconds, and during that time, really get into thinking. Let your mind run with the first thought that pops up, and then let it proliferate. Count things or describe them, verbalizing your thoughts with an internal commentary. Count your breaths if you want, or name sounds you hear or sensations you are feeling. It feels a bit unusual, and it's actually quite tiring, but keep at it.

When the timer goes off, we set it for another ninety seconds, and in that second ninety seconds, we stop. The harder we think in the first ninety seconds, the easier it is to stop in the second. We hang there, thought-free.

In being thought-free we notice something. Awareness does not stop, even though thought does. Of course, the moment a commentary starts — such as, "Wow, I am without thoughts!" — that commentary is itself a thought! But we can — initially only for brief moments, but then extending second by second — just rest in thought-free awareness.

If you like, you can repeat the practice for another two ninety-second periods, or as many times as you like.

Sitting in Silence

This is a very simple meditation trick. Purely practical. Set a timer and think deliberately for ninety seconds. Think about things or name and describe them. Immerse yourself in a full commentary in this manner. Keep on thinking hard, even when normally in meditation you would want to stop. And then drop it all. Just rest, silent.

This technique enables us to get alongside thinking and then drop it. The contrast between thinking and not thinking becomes apparent. And practicing this gives us the taste of thought-free awareness. If you want to relax stiff shoulders, what do you do? Tense your shoulders and then let them go. This is exactly the same idea. We think deliberately — think, think, think, think, think — and then let go. The harder we think, the more total the letting go will be.

Meditating like this, even if for a moment, can give us a glimpse of the stability underlying all aspects of our experience, the stability that is always there. It is sometimes called "the ground." It is there within thinking and remains when we stop thinking. We only do the exercise of thinking deliberately and then stopping to make it more apparent. Often the glimpse is very partial because we immediately conceptualize it and so start thinking again. But in becoming aware of thought-free awareness itself, we get a little glimpse of a ground that is repeatedly obscured by our web of thought — that narrative map full of names and ideas that we have been referring to.

A major goal in meditation is to remain steady in a mind that is free from reflexive reactivity, and the conceptual thought that proliferates from it. Such a mind is not obscured moment to moment by the subject-object world map we construct for ourselves. One could say the goal is to find our natural intelligence that is free from all the hints and echoes we otherwise carry around with us. Although we might find thinking deliberately somewhat strange, nonetheless if we do it, when we stop thinking, even for a moment, we have a brief experience of clarity where we can almost feel our thoughts stirring.

Our sensory apparatus is always producing inputs, and we're triggered by them to make responses. But before those responses arise, there is something else. Becoming aware of this is a real key to meditation. Don't try to control it, or extend it, or analyze it. In itself this stillness is vast, pervasive, and clear. We make the mistake of trying to capture it as an experience, to compress it into a little conceptual box, to recognize it, know it, and then abide there as if we were a watcher of it all. Such an attempt will always frustrate any real progress, for this thought-free stillness is always present even when there are thoughts happening. Realizing this is a key to successful meditation.

This exercise is a preface for what we could call *vipassana*, clear seeing. *Vipassana* requires *shamata*, but it requires the right kind of *shamata*. Here we access *shamata* by deliberately thinking, naming, analyzing anything we can feel or hear. Name it, count it, think about it. And then in the second ninety seconds, drop the naming. Rest there for a moment. Of course, thoughts will start to arise. For a moment you can feel them tugging at you, wanting you to engage with the proliferation of thought. Instead, remain there, thought-free.

Questions and Comments

I've noticed that when I start naming something, there is a sense of me doing it. But when I drop the naming in the second half of the practice, not thinking or not naming is much more neutral. I don't get a sense of "I."

There's a big explanation for this: it's all to do with world construction, how we construct experience, how we make the world. We have talked previously about labeling, naming, and how we identify elements of our experience in this manner. But there is another element of our experience that is also named: "me," "I," "myself." When there are no names, there is no namer either. No "me," no "I," no "mine." So then the question is, "If there's no me, how do I act?"

Strangely, we are surrounded by the answer to this question. When we see true excellence, whether it is in performance, or art, or sports, that performer, artist, or athlete has overcome their sense of "me." Think of a concert pianist in the middle of a great performance. The piano player is totally in the spirit of the performance, within it, absorbed. It is the same with the great athlete or anyone whose excellence we can witness. There is no "me" there.

I have to say, it was exhausting trying to keep thinking going. And I wonder if you can suggest further reading on this subject.

It is hard to think deliberately like that, isn't it? Normally our thoughts randomly proliferate without our involvement, but when we think deliberately, it is much more of an effort!

The problem with reading about things like this is that we aggregate ideas from reading books, which are always seen through the lens of our prior experience. How else can we know what the words mean except through whatever a prior experience tells us they mean? What is required here, though, is somewhat different. In meditation we need to open the door to experience itself. Words are not experiences; they are labels that point to experiences. But if we haven't had those experiences, the words can be worse than useless because they are without a reference, requiring us to imagine what they might be referring to, rather than referring to an actual experience. To return to our chocolate analogy, this would be like claiming to be an expert in different types of chocolate based on reading alone, without ever having tasted chocolate! What we are trying to do here is to give very simple, nontechnical guidance to encourage direct engagement. Once we've had the experience, then the words no longer mislead us because they refer to something we actually know.

Because experience is so important, it has often been said that the perfect student of meditation has no expectations, as if they had no education whatsoever. But in our contemporary culture it's effectively illegal to be without education. We don't have access to that kind of cognitive naivete, so we have to be clever and use our education sneakily to gather direct experience. This is why this "contrast meditation," in which we think and then not think, and other similar meditations are so valuable. They allow us to directly experience states that are otherwise covered over by our pervasive reactivity.

Only read on once you have done
your seven days!

CHAPTER ELEVEN

Vipassana 101

Last week we talked about how thoughts can disturb us. If thoughts disturb you in your meditation, you can get ahead of them by thinking deliberately. We're not used to thinking deliberately because thoughts normally happen to us, rather than the other way around. This is because we do not notice the arising of thought, only the proliferation of thought that happens once thought has been triggered. As a result of this, we normally think that thoughts are a problem, and we should shut them down. This is a limited view, however. It is more useful to see that thoughts are not a problem — they are merely a feature of our mental activity. The real problem is our reaction to them. But once we get ahead of thoughts by thinking deliberately, we can work with our reactions.

When we stop thinking, we find ourselves in a state of calmness. Initially we may only be able to access that state by thinking hard and then stopping, but as we get used to it, increasingly we will be able to access thought-free awareness at will. Furthermore, having got a taste for it, if we are attentive, we can find that calmness while we are thinking as well. It's not that thoughts replace a state of thought-free calmness. It's rather that our thoughts pull us away from such states of calmness. You could say that thoughts obscure the calm state, like clouds obscuring the sun — that our bright clarity is obscured by the endless proliferation that thoughts engender.

Since thoughts rise and fall in a continuous progression, it is not the arising of thoughts that disturbs us so much as our reactions to them. Like impressions arising at every other gate, our reflexive reactivity is what causes likes, dislikes, irritations, obligations, and commentaries that cloud over our natural clarity. As we develop our *shamata*, as we learn to put down our turbulent glass of water and overcome our reflexive reactivity, this turbulence begins to settle by itself. We can then begin to experience *vipassana*; we can then begin to see clearly.

Among the most important elements of our experience in seeing clearly are thoughts themselves. After all, thoughts are the most dominant element of our mental continuum, but unlike impressions arising in our gates of vision, hearing, taste, touch, and smell, they arise inside us, seemingly without origin. But where do they come from? They must arise from somewhere. After all, they are not fixed — they rise and fall like waves on the sea. Furthermore, where do they go? They're not with us forever. They disappear. We forget stuff all the time. Thoughts come. Thoughts go. While we are in the middle of a thought, it can be completely engrossing. But then it is over — gone completely. This is a somewhat enigmatic phenomenon. Thoughts are rather like having a strange houseguest. They keep arriving in our house without warning and taking it over, and then they disappear — gone.

To address the inquiry of where thoughts come from and where they go is really *vipassana* 101. But it is only possible if the questioning itself is not conceptual. This may seem like a strange statement. Can't we merely "look within" and find an answer to this puzzle? As must have become clear over the past ten weeks, such an act of looking is itself a thought. We cannot merely use a thought to ask a thought where thoughts come from! There was a school of introspectionism in the early part of the twentieth century inspired by the work of William James that attempted to do this, and it failed utterly. In trying to look in this manner, we bring our preconceptions with us and get nowhere. But here our *shamata* base can help us. Indeed, one could say that understanding where thoughts come from and where they go is a graphic illustration of why a base of calm clarity is required to understand ourselves and how we react to events.

To address where thoughts come from and where they go, our first step is to be quiet, calm, and clear. In such a state, the state we have been working steadily to become familiar with over the past weeks, thoughts will arise continually. But when a thought arises, we simply observe its beginning with the implicit question, "Where did this thought come from?" This is not a question that is asked; it is more like a stance of inquiry. Like an artist who looks at a scene to capture something of it on a canvas, we seek *insight* into the question rather than a simple answer. Indeed, sometimes *vipassana* is called "insight meditation" for this reason. To practice *vipassana*, then, is to use our intent, our clear determination, while resting in a state of calm.

As a thought arises, we can know it has arisen, and experience an immediate itch to react to it — to become immersed in what it "means." It is our impulse toward immersion that triggers the proliferation, the obscuration that takes us away from calm clarity and becomes disturbing and exhausting. So what happens if we do not enter a relationship with the arising thought; what happens if we don't react to it? We are still here! We don't need to be pulled into a reaction like "I'm aware of this thought." The moment we have the idea that we are aware of thoughts, we are in one! We have become engaged, a "looker." Here we begin to realize a profound fruit of clear seeing, of *vipassana*. The narrative we live within winds us into itself the whole time. It's always looping. Thoughts arise, and it is almost as if they have hooks on them, like Velcro. Our internal story is waiting there to catch those hooks, to engender associations, to engage us. That's how we get engrossed, entangled, knotted up in the narrative, whatever our narrative is. Being a "spiritual person" is no protection! But for three minutes, we can find a way of not being tangled up. If we remain untangled, we can see the whole process; indeed, if we can have clear seeing, *vipassana*, of that, we won't get tangled up in the narrative in the first place, and thoughts will arise and pass away all by themselves.

So how do thoughts end? This is also a valuable insight. Thoughts come and go, but their going is often lost on us, because they have triggered a proliferation of other thoughts, so the ending of the first thought is lost in the arising of all the other thoughts it triggered. This makes it look like thoughts are continuous, that they are some sort of powerful foe we have to vanquish to be free of them. Again, in calm clarity, if the first thought is seen without triggering proliferation, its ending emerges. But this is a bit like asking where mist ends or where clouds end. There is a fading, a gradual thinning, no clear point. What gives substance to the whole experience of thought is the proliferation from one thought to another in an ever-expanding array. Once our reflexive reactivity is understood, once our base of calm clarity is inhabited, individual thoughts arise and pass like birds flying in an empty sky.

EXERCISE
Where Do Thoughts Come from and Where Do They Go?

Rest in calm clarity for your three minutes this week, whether you achieve this through thinking and then not thinking, or resting with a smile, or any of the previous exercises. Thoughts arise. Simply rest with the questions, "Where do they come from?" and "Do they come from anywhere at all?" Normally we are not aware of the beginning of a thought because thoughts need a certain intensity to come into our awareness, and we tend to react to them reflexively and find ourselves traveling with them before we are aware that they have arisen at all. But by establishing a state of calm, we can intend to see their beginning. As they arise, they become clear to us.

After a few moments, another attitudinal question is also helpful: "Where do thoughts go?" We know that they end, but normally we aren't aware of their ending. It is also fruitful to be interested in this, even if it seems kind of nebulous. One thought ends, another begins — it feels continuous in a fuzzy kind of way. But through resting clearly, we can allow thoughts to arise, and then stay with them and see where they go and what happens as they stop. Does another thought immediately come? What happens there? In seeing their ending, rather than their proliferation, we see them evaporate back into the spaciousness of calm clarity from whence they came.

Take this stance of inquiry, and rest there for three minutes a day.

The Three Times of Thought

In this first exercise of *vipassana*, we use our clear seeing to watch where thoughts come from and where they go. Of course, if we know where thoughts come from, and we know where thoughts go, we'll know where they are between arising and going away. This awareness of the three times of thoughts — of their arising in the past, their abiding in the present, and their dissolution in the future — comes like a wave on a body of water. This meditation is of great value because thoughts are the ubiquitous bedfellows of our experience. It opens the door to another revealing question: "What are thoughts?" Most dictionary definitions are of little value because they merely refer thoughts themselves to other thoughts. Like the experience of the taste of chocolate, once we experience thoughts, rather than merely allow them to take us over, we can generate a clear comprehension. *Shamata* smoothly moves into *vipassana*. On a calm foundation, clear seeing is there.

Questions and Comments

I feel like I've been doing some form of this for a while now. What I have noticed is how attached I am to my thoughts. It is like Velcro — really strong.

To see the base of this attachment is to begin to deeply penetrate the narrative structure in which we live. Our identity, our sense of self, is tied to our thoughts. Our thoughts make references, giving us locations by which we live. This is what makes them magnetic, sticky. This is why we become bundled up with them so readily.

I have trouble with rambling thoughts. I can notice thoughts in a passive way, like waves on the ocean, but I find it's hard to get a fix on where they come from and where they go.

This is why last week's exercise is so valuable. If you find that your thought machine is running along seemingly out of your control, get ahead of it. Decide you are going to promote thought. Spend a few minutes thinking deliberately. Then stop. The thought train gets interrupted. You took control of it. Then you can see thoughts arising and ceasing without that rolling proliferation that before felt so automatic. Like the judo move, you're basically going along with it instead of resisting. Whatever the thought, any thought will do. It doesn't matter. You need to get ahead of that thinking mechanism by deliberately thinking. Then stop. When you stop, at least for a while, it will be quiet. If you like, you can try practicing last week's exercise for another week and then return to this week's, and see if it's any easier.

Is thinking always verbal? It seems like we pay attention to the sentences, the voice, or the words.

That's an interesting question for you to ask yourself. Are thoughts always in words, or can we get to a pre-verbal element, which is still a thought but hasn't quite matured itself into words? What about images? Are they also thoughts?

I had been under the impression that sensations triggered the beginning of thoughts, but while I did this practice, it felt like there was no direct connection between the physical sensation and the thought that arose from it. Is that incorrect?

Beginning to see the arising of thoughts is *vipassana*, but it is not that a physical sensation or internal stirring expresses a thought directly. They can be triggered by such events, but their content is sometimes quite random. If you really get into your mental process, you realize you are constructing a narrative the whole time from these haphazard elements of experience, as with dreaming. Thoughts are arising tangentially, bouncing off one impression or another. It's that we have an internal referent that keeps us feeling like we are going somewhere, a destination, like we know for sure what we are doing. This is because through it all we have a plan, a narrative structure of "me in the world" that selects from all these internal voices and creates a coherent picture. Once we develop some insight, some *vipassana*, we begin to see that this narrative is a selection, a small subset of what is actually happening in and around us.

You said to look at our thoughts, but I'm not sure how to do that.

The word *look* is a little misleading. I don't mean to literally *look, look, look!* That is too conceptual. We need to be there lightly. If we look too hard, we merely conceptualize. It's more like a sideways glance rather than a stare. But if we maintain a state of *shamata*, our looking becomes effortless. If our looking interrupts our *shamata*, then it is conceptual — it is just looking that is guided by the thought of something to see. The looking we are trying to find is the looking that arises within calm clarity and does not disturb it. Then we see what actually is, without any preconception whatsoever.

Isn't that the difference between looking and seeing? Seeing doesn't have effort.

That might be a helpful distinction. But these are all terms that really only make sense if you experience them. Words are clothed with meaning through experience.

I'm not sure how I fit into this. I am dyslexic. I mainly experience things through pictures. There are no words sometimes, just pictures.

Thoughts are as much imagery as they are verbal. They get words associated with them. Thinking in images is no issue at all. The associations that are triggered, one to the next, are generated in much the same way.

What about the proliferation you have been talking about?

We can have a discourse in images. One image can trigger another. Indeed, that often happens when we dream. These are all inquiries we can make about our own mental experiences. But don't take my word for it. Try it for yourself.

Only read on once you have done
your seven days!

CHAPTER TWELVE

The Display

Vipassana has gotten a lot of airtime in the past twenty years or so because it's become synonymous with meditation. This is a partial view, however. Meditation techniques that involve breath watching or noting sensations are primarily *shamata*, which leads to *vipassana* as a result. Most of the instructions you might receive actually teach *shamata*. *Shamata* is something you can practice. I hope you are beginning to develop this faculty of calm clarity, for through practicing *shamata*, you will have the ability to have a calm and clear base from which to experience *vipassana*, to see clearly. In our normal experience we all suffer from not having a calm base, and so our ability to clearly see our experience escapes us.

In order to better understand *vipassana*, it can be valuable to gather a little background information — what we might be looking for. This background is not unlike reading a guidebook before visiting a foreign country. It points out things that we might want to take note of, introducing us to a bit of the history and perhaps encouraging us to explore certain things that otherwise we might miss. But when we go on a trip it can be a bit depressing to find tourists holding their guidebooks up to their faces and not seeing anything else! For them, background reading has replaced their experience. Experience is always beyond such information, no matter how detailed it is. All the background information does is point to where we might look. As mentioned earlier, think of walking up a mountain and meeting someone coming down. They say, "Around the next corner is a great view of a glacier." With that suggestion they're giving us background information. We go around the next corner. We don't have to look at the glacier, but they were pointing out that there is something nice to look at. It's a way of guiding, but not requiring, our attention.

What is the background to what we're looking at here? It is this: While sensations and impressions are arriving continuously at our six gates, we interpret them through a preformed representation we call the world, all the time. We don't remember ourselves doing this, because our memory works by using this representation as a base. But if we look in real time, as things are happening, rather than remembering them as having happened, what we find is different in important ways. One of the most important is that the referent to ourselves, that label of "I," "me," or "mine" that is used to assign meaning to what happens to us, is not present in the events themselves. Rather, it is recorded in a narrative structure in which the events that happened are organized by reference to those labels of "I," "me," or "mine" along with an internal time stamp in our recollection of events. That is how our memory places us in the events it records, and how it orders those records into a coherent narrative.

This systematic illusion that we are normally unaware of is a major element in the generation of disquiet and suffering, the emotional turmoil that can be such a feature of our lives. This is not to claim that all experience is an illusion. But we do need to remind ourselves that our experience of any sense object or event is always an interpretation, displayed to us as a "thing" or occurrence that happens to or is noticed by "me," whereas the actuality of the thing or event, seen in the clear light of *vipassana*, turns out to be significantly different. In the event as it actually happened, in the actuality of it, there was no thing or "me" there at all.

Wow! What a discovery! And as briefly discussed in the first week of our exploration, the display we generate of our experience is nearly a half second behind the events that give rise to it. We experience the display as continuous and smooth, however. This is why we do not normally realize that it's a half second behind events; it is only when reaction time is demonstrated, or optical illusions shown, that we begin to see that our experience is being constructed, moment to moment. So how can we experience a *vipassana* of this situation? How are we going to see it? We can't go outside to look. There is no outside to look from. So how can we begin to access something that might show us how the display is generated?

Our endeavor is to try to see the display of mind itself. We want to experience a *vipassana* of it somehow. Our difficulty is that impressions are arising at our six sense gates continuously, and in reaction to them the display is being continuously generated, moment to moment. Here, too, our practice of contrast meditation can help us. It is based on the simple principle that, as mentioned earlier, if you want to relax a muscle the best way is to contract it and then let go. It is very difficult to relax something unless it's coming from a state of tension. Contrast used in this way can also be a powerful tool in *vipassana*. We can use contrast meditation to help us recognize the difference between the display and the sense impressions that generate it.

We have been doing this implicitly in all the meditations we have practiced in recent weeks, but now it is time to deliberately open up a chink in the seamless facade within which we normally live. In this regard, of all the six sense gates — hearing, seeing, touching, tasting, smelling, and mind — the easiest to work with is hearing.

Hearing is interesting here because it plays a major role in constructing the narrative of our experience. It is often treated as a secondary sense in our normal awareness, and we don't usually realize how important a role it plays. Sound plays a fundamental function in reifying the display, making it real. Try this sometime: watch TV with the sound off. A muted TV show becomes just a series of images; it is very hard to work out what is going on. But turn the sound back on, and you get sucked right back into the story or spectacle. Furthermore, radio, podcasts, and audiobooks, where there are no visual images at all, can actually be more immersive and evocative than TV. Hearing makes meaning in a way we normally do not realize.

EXERCISE
Sitting by a Window

Here is a very simple contrast meditation. Sit near an open window somewhere where there is sound — say, of traffic, birds calling, people talking, or whatever else is going on. (If opening a window is not an option, you could easily do this with indoor sounds, as long as there are sounds happening continually. Or, if the weather is nice, you could sit outdoors instead of by a window.) Set a timer for ninety seconds. Close your eyes and concentrate on those sounds. For that first minute and a half, sit and allow the sounds to wash over you. Don't name them, don't locate them; let the sounds happen, without analyzing them in any way.

Then, running the timer for another ninety seconds, in that time try to identify every sound you hear — what it is, where it's coming from, whether it is behind, in front, or to the left or right of you. Try to locate and identify it precisely.

So in the first period, we do not identify the sounds or their location, and then in the second period, we practice identifying. If you wish to repeat the exercise, reverse the order: in the first ninety seconds identify all the sounds, then in the second let the sounds wash over you.

You can experience a *vipassana* of the difference between these two modalities. It is very striking. In the period without identification, there is only sound. If you allow the sound to happen, neither naming nor locating it, it can even be hard to tell whether it is coming from inside or outside of you. You might hear your ears ringing, for example. But if you relax into the sound, where is it coming from? The second period, when we identify sounds, is entirely different. Here we are clearly located, the center of the world, and all the sounds are happening in relation to us. The contrast between these two is a primary insight of *vipassana*. It's the seeing of our situation as being composed of name and form. Forms are made from sense impressions, in this case the sounds at the ear gate, and our naming is the process of identifying those sounds as particular things. By alternating identifying and not identifying, we can experience a *vipassana* of our knowing function; by turning our attention to the sense gates themselves, we can see how we make a world of experience with ourselves at the center of it.

Another fascinating insight arises from this contrast meditation. In our first period, when we do not locate or identify the impressions arising at the sound gate, there is no strong sense of self. Do it for long enough, and the sense of "I," of being a person in the world, slowly fades away. All there is, is experience itself. But in the second period the reverse is the case. By locating and identifying sound, "I" am clearly defined, with boundaries that belong to "me," and by extension, things that are "mine." Could these three terms be merely labels by which we organize our experience of the world? Reflect on your ninety-second meditations after your practice. Is "I" present in both of them or only one?

Seeing Sense Input

We rarely experience sound, sight, taste, smell, or touch, per se. We always have ourselves as some central point, with our past knowledge of these sensations. To begin to see how we construct our experience, this contrast meditation is very valuable. It starts us working on penetrating the display bubble within which we live our lives. Whatever sounds are around you, close your eyes, open a window, and listen.

If you're really brave, sit on a park bench, close your eyes, and do this exercise. (Go with a friend, though, so you are not actually in any danger.) Try it — this can be very revealing. Having allowed sounds to simply manifest in the first period, for the second ninety seconds, really work to identify what's happening, and see the difference in your psychological state between these two ways of processing sense inputs. In the second period you may get all kinds of additional fantasies that will proliferate, such as perhaps interpreting a strange sound as that of a bus running out of control straight toward you. They can be very striking but are entirely a production of our internal state. You are learning to see your own display, a *vipassana*, having established the calm base of *shamata*.

Questions and Comments

Eyes open or closed? Does it matter?

It doesn't really, because we are not concentrating on the eye gate. If we have our eyes open and we are not looking at anything in particular, that's fine, as long as we aren't looking specifically. On the other hand, if you find having your eyes closed is easier, that is also fine. But this is not a trance meditation. We're not trying to go deep with the concentration, which can happen with our eyes closed. We're merely listening passively, and then by contrast, actively.

I found it a little hard to switch. The earlier contrast meditation, trying to think and then not, was clearer and more distinct. This one seems to be about trying to think about hearing.

In the first half you drop all identification as if you were sunbathing on a beach with stuff going on around you. In the second half of the practice, when you are identifying sounds, the idea is that you're almost like a detective or secret agent — you are really listening, trying to identify what is going on. In that sense you are thinking, but really you are investigating the sounds you are hearing. Can you experience the difference between those two states?

I found in the second part I was hunting down the source. It was leading me into interesting questions: "Is the motor big or small?" and so on. That was fun for my mind.

What we're trying to do in *vipassana* is to become conscious of the construction of perception. One of the techniques to bring this into awareness is to over-construct and then under-construct. This abrupt change helps us see the difference. What happened to us during our childhood is that we gradually emerged into a construct, elaborated by our education. Consequently we very rarely see this process because the construct didn't arrive all at once. It gradually accumulated until we emerged as an adult in a world. In our meditation, we are trying to make that world-making process visible. The construct is pervasive and reflexive; it is hard to see. We have to find tools, chinks in the armor, gaps where we start seeing it. To see through the display in which we live, we need to break through to something that is almost beyond analysis, whether we do so through contrast meditation, as here, or through direct seeing. But if we are able to develop our *shamata* to the point where we have real stability, we will see without question. Once our habitual reflexivity no longer pulls us away, we will see. This is *vipassana*.

Only read on once you have done
your seven days!

CHAPTER THIRTEEN

Not Doing

We spend our life in a dialogue. The dialogue we have is based on a set of words and concepts that provide an explanation of our experience. This narrative creates a continuity in which we live, but it doesn't take a moment to realize that none of us actually experience "the world." In fact, all the other beings and processes that surround us are so myriad in number and complexity that such an experience is quite literally impossible. If we were to go into our backyard and try to work out all the causal chains of events occurring there, it would take us forever. There are thousands and thousands of causal chains happening at the same time. Imagine every person alive in their own story, and all the different atmospheric conditions; the microscopic dramas of insects, mammals, and birds; the depths of the oceans; all the family dynamics and dramas; the sociopolitical settings — the list is almost endless. Although we all talk about "the world," what we are really referring to is our own bubble of ideas and concepts by which we make sense of the experience that is happening to us.

When we see a pair of glasses, for example, we name them in our mind as "glasses," and quite often the next thing we might think is "my glasses." With that personal pronoun comes an association web of the memories we have. We might remember when we bought them. Are they good or bad? Perhaps we need to replace them. Do we like the frames? Remember how expensive they were? Many elements link any object we come across to our causal continuum.

This continuum is not only names and memories, though. It also contains strong injunctions, opinions about right and wrong, views that fix our experience and conform our responses. Ultimately, through our responses, we seek wisdom, which is the ability to respond authentically to the actual circumstances we encounter. In this regard, our established views and opinions can act as an obstacle. Seeing them clearly enables us to make better choices.

We can also work to prepare ourselves for this seeing, by doing what one could call a *pre-passana*, a preparation for seeing, which is a simple exercise that is surprisingly liberating with regard to the causal narrative. As mentioned above, events are happening around us all the time, many of them highly polarizing in the political and sports arenas, particularly with our twenty-four-hour news cycle. Because we have highly charged narratives, we generally find ourselves firmly on one side of the fence or the other with regard to them. Whatever side of the fence we are on, our preparation for *vipassana*, our *pre-passana*, is to practice being happy if the other guy, or the other side, wins. Whatever arguments we may have as to why the other side is wrong, just as an exercise, we can put them aside and feel happy that the other side prevails.

This exercise is not to give credence to wrong views, but rather to wriggle some freedom from our own. It is the prison of opinion we are interested in, not the rights and wrongs of a particular opinion itself. The causal continuum in which we live is both a construct we have made to explain our lives and, equally, the boundary within which we live our lives. Since my view is the only one I've got, if I'm addicted to my view I'm only going to be looking through a tiny little window at what might be possible. Working to deconstruct it is important if we are to achieve freedom. Otherwise we see only a fraction of what might be out there for human beings.

So the *pre-passana* exercise is to imagine right now that the other guy or the other side is winning, and we are happy about it. We are delighted that they are winning. This is great news. We are really happy. The happier, the better. The immediate sensation is one of freedom and joy.

When we think about this, it seems like it's going to be difficult. It seems distasteful to want the bad guy to win because we know he's a bad guy. He's done a million bad things. But the exercise is to be happy at the success he is having, as if it's a great thing. If you can do this, if you can overcome the distaste of celebrating your opponent's success, see how you feel. It's like a weight that's lifted off. For a moment, the weight of the view that you had lifts. This is a *pre-passana*, a trick that for a moment frees us from our weighty opinions. It doesn't have to affect our actions. It only affects our outlook.

Our views arise because we live our lives in a nested set of stories; sometimes it is called a "superego," which could be understood as the background against which we live — the overarching story within which we live our individual story. Each of us has such a background, made from family and societal heritage and including elements like where we were born, our job, things that have happened to us, and so on. Nations also have such a narrative. The British Empire still informs British identity, as American exceptionalism informs the United States. It can be hard to work out what these insidious sentiments are, but they influence and create deep feelings in us about what is right and wrong.

This nested set of stories is there when we open our eyes in the morning, runs with us right through the day, and continues when we dream at night, with only brief moments when there are gaps between one element and another. Normally we can't see this storytelling narrative, but we can make it an object for our *vipassana*. We may have developed stability, seen where thoughts come from and go, and even experienced being within a narrative and dropping it. But to really experience *vipassana*, we need to stop. It is only then that the full narrative structure in which we are embedded becomes visible to us.

EXERCISE
The Stop

Having done the *pre-passana* of imagining the bad guy winning to get a little bit free of our opinions, we are now going to create a circumstance for *vipassana*. The circumstance is to stop. This meditation is unusual. For a moment, a few seconds at a time, we stop everything — stop moving, stop looking, stop hearing — just stop. We can either do it randomly or on a timer. If we do it on a timer, it is best to forget we are on a timer. We're not stopping on the hour, for example. That would be putting a narrative on it. Set an alarm on your phone for some period, long enough to forget it is there — say, three hours and fifteen minutes. When the alarm goes off, stop. Stop everything for a few seconds, no longer. Then move on again. Do that maybe three times a day.

Don't hang on to the stop. Don't make the stop anything other than a stop. When we stop, nothing happens. We don't know anything. We don't see anything. We don't look at anything. We stop physically and mentally.

Then we go back to our business. The mistake is to try to make the stop into something more than it actually is. It's just a stop.

You will notice very quickly that when you stop the world rushes by, just for a moment. It's a weird sensation. It's as if we're floating along in a shallow river and everything is floating along beside us, so there is no sensation of the water moving; and then we stand up. Suddenly we feel the water flowing past us. Since we are not moving but the river and all the things floating in it keep moving, for a moment we see this stuff floating past. That is our world — what is moving along with us. Do that, then relax back into the flow. That flow is the narrative structure in which we live.

Stepping Out of the Narrative

When we stop we don't disappear. If we can stop three times a day, though, by the end of a week we will have an experience of the narrative in which we live. We'll be surprised how life goes on. One thing leads to the next. This is the causal continuum into which we are born, where we spend all our lives. But the stop exercise provides a moment of transition when, for that moment, we are stepping out of the game. This allows a brief window of *vipassana*. Our entire cognitive apparatus is invested in the narrative — all our words and intentions are associated with it. This is why we cannot achieve *vipassana* by saying, "I'm going to see!" The moment we see, we've created a narrative structure. The problem is that we've used the word *I*. Our language bewitches us. Our task is to become free of the bewitchment of language. For this, we stop. That is the one power we always have.

The Indian tradition uses a knot to describe the weave in which we're embedded. We're embedded in a structure. Our ability to clearly see our situation bleeds through to a vaster understanding about the nature of our being — what we actually are. It goes beyond the categories of culture. If we ask ourselves, "How do I know where I am right now?" we can only give an answer because of causal continuity. We remember what we were doing a moment before, how it led up to our current position. But we have no actual knowledge of where we are right now. It is an inference, based upon a narrative we have created, a storyline full of causes and reasons within which we are embedded. We normally say, "I'm here because I was there before." This means that the basis of our experience is an inference based on a flow, rather than something actual, based on direct knowledge of our circumstance. Were it actual, we would no longer be in the flow because we would be here, right now.

It is a good exercise to think to oneself, "What happened a moment ago? Where's that moment gone?" It is quite literally gone. It's not coming back. We look at animals and think, "Oh, these poor things. They really don't know what's going on. They're nibbling grass.

They don't realize what life really is." But really we are in the same boat. We are comfortable in our lives, yet moment to moment things disappear. What we did this morning has gone. It's not coming back. What is that? What is the true nature of our life and situation?

A powerful way to gain experience of these questions is to stop. Stop everything, just for a moment. You won't disappear. You won't fall into a hole and have to pop out again. The more you can stop and then restart, the better. The cleaner you can be about the stop, the more clearly you can see.

Furthermore, having come to the stop, do by all means combine it with any of the earlier three-minute practices, so your calm base becomes ever more firmly established. You could even do one of the preceding practices on each day of the week, along with the stop at random points in the day. Slowly but surely, we are becoming artists of our own perception.

Questions and Comments

I don't know if I really stopped or just imagined that I did.

Just stop. When you doubt that you are stopping, stop right there and then, in the middle of the question you are asking yourself about whether you stopped. The stop is a non-action. It's not an imagination. When the thought "How do I know if I'm imagining this?" comes, you can stop again, right in the middle of that thought. Don't give that doubt the airtime it's asking for. You need to stop in the face of it. The stop itself has an authentic feeling that is not magic — it is actual. The answer is in the doing, or more properly, in the not doing of the stop. We're not a computer program. We're not the ghost in the machine. We are the machine. It's a knowing machine. There is no conflict between being and knowing. Being is knowing, knowing is being — it's the same thing. It's non-dual.

Sometimes when I stop, I feel I am staring and trying to fix my experience as unmoving or something. I realize that is not right, so I try to use soft eyes to overcome it.

All that staring and fixing is abiding. The easiest way to overcome abiding is to stop within the abiding. Notice your impulse to fix, that attempt to freeze everything, and then stop there. You can use *shamata* as your base and then stop there. Then you are stopping within abiding itself.

This moment when we stop seems valuable. You said to do it and then forget it. Is the narrative inevitable? Is there anything valuable to examine at that point?

This is the irony of spiritual realization. The moment you try to analyze the stop, you have conceptualized it. If we try writing about the stop in a diary, trying to find out what it means and thinking about it, all we do is reincorporate it back into the narrative that our stopping momentarily allowed us to escape from. There are other ways of diarizing, but the stop is a non-doing, a stepping out of the continuity of our life.

Our mental apparatus is always trying to make a narrative for us. It is a protective mechanism designed to help us navigate an uncertain world. But ultimately we want to be free of views, so we can respond to any situation with fresh insight, unfettered by prior opinion. How can we be free of views if we review everything? By all means, experience the stop. But then go right back to your normal business as if it never happened.

Only read on once you have done
your seven days!

CHAPTER FOURTEEN

Getting Off the Cushion

We end this fourteen-week journey with finding avenues to take *vipassana* into action. Generally our level of consciousness about what we're doing is relatively low. That is to say, most of our activities are unconscious. We only analyze what we're doing when it doesn't fit with our expectations. For example, becoming proficient in a skill enables us to paradoxically forget that we are doing it. Whether it is learning a musical instrument or speaking a new language, as we become more expert, we become less aware of what we are doing rather than more. Recall when you first learned to drive. You were acutely aware of your hands on the wheel and the positions of the pedals and gear shift. Your driving was conscious but tentative. As you became more familiar, these sensations faded into the background. If you spent your entire time worrying where your hands were on the steering wheel, you wouldn't be a very good driver. Similarly, when we get up out of a chair we don't think, "I am moving my legs into this position." It is completely unconscious. We're not aware of ourselves making these motions. Another example is giving a speech at someone's wedding. If you stand up to make a speech and you're conscious of yourself doing it, it's going to be a terrible speech. The only way to make a good speech is to completely forget that you're making a speech and engage with the audience. The moment we have any self-consciousness of what we are doing, we become tongue-tied.

What is happening in all these examples of learning a new skill? In developing a skill, we replace conscious awareness of what we are doing with a map. This shorthand makes us far more efficient. Unfortunately, though, if we have incorporated any bad habits into that map, it can be extremely difficult to eradicate them.

Now let's consider what happens when we arise from our meditation cushion. Sitting there, we can stabilize our *shamata*, follow sensations with *vitaka* and *vicara*, and become aware of our situation. But when we get up off our cushion, we have to learn to continue that awareness without becoming a tongue-tied beginner, like the novice giving the best man's speech or the driver in training. We're so used to reflexively relying on a map that when we cease relying on it we find ourselves unable to function. We want to go back to our cushion, sit quietly, and not move. But to truly experience a *vipassana* of any situation, we must learn to go beyond our reliance on knowing what we are doing, into a spontaneous interaction with events as they arise.

One way to address this is to take the stop into motion. The stop we practiced last week was a cessation. We simply stopped and for a moment watched our narrative world and the actions associated with it flow past us. What were we stopping, however? As we become familiar with this exercise, we begin to realize that what we were stopping is our engagement with the narrative itself. For a moment we stepped back from the map and stopped.

This stepping back can also be practiced in action. Take a simple sweep of the hand, for example. Normally when we move our hand, we are unconscious of the movement because we are focused on a goal, like "I want to pick up my cup of coffee." We are not conscious of moving our hand, because we are focusing on the task ahead of us. Because of this, the movement we make to pick up the coffee cup is overlooked. Using our map metaphor, we have given up our experience of a body and replaced it with an intentional map. But this is a process we can reverse. We can learn to remain aware of a movement as we make it and get used to the feeling of inhabiting the movement itself. We suddenly realize we can move within the stop. We are not obligated to sit stationary like a Buddha statue or a piece of wood. We soon realize that the stop can work as well in motion as it does in stillness.

It feels strange to inhabit motion in this manner. We need to see clearly what is happening here too. It leads to a major discovery. As we learn to stop in motion, we realize that even in the simplest hand wave, there is no "I" there! There is just motion. The "I," the focal point around which all our experience seemingly revolves, is revealed as a map reference! When we stop using the map, the reference point is not there, any more than the altitude markers printed on a topographical map actually exist on the hillside path we are walking up.

Taking the stop into action opens the door to a different way of being. Our experience of this seems tentative and fragile at first. All our learning, all our history, struggles, successes, and failures are screaming at us that the "I" is a necessary factor. Surely the narrative by which we have navigated our lives is all about "I," is it not? Here our *vipassana* shows us something different. Over the previous thirteen weeks we have built a base from which we can see clearly. And in clear seeing, the "I" is revealed to be part of the story, an actor on the screen, rather than part of the actuality upon which the story is based. But we need to start slowly here, practicing simple exercises that allow us to take our *vipassana* into action. As our confidence grows, we realize that the absence of "I" is true in all circumstances. When we stop, we do not disappear. In the same way, when we realize the "I" is not part of experience itself, we do not become unable to act. Far from it, in fact. The door to freedom beckons; actuality lies before us.

One might ask whether this is a big, momentous restructuring of our experience or a small one. Surprisingly, it is the latter. The sense of identity that seems so essential for any activity does not exist in the activity itself. Nothing really changes at the level of action. The change happens at the level of narrative, the level of what our actions mean. "Mean to whom?" one might ask. Mean to us, of course! So our sense of selfhood is required to provide a sense of meaning... to itself! This is the self-referential loop of identity our *vipassana* finally reveals. And as we cut through it, untie the knot, and get off our cushion, a previously unimaginable freedom beckons.

EXERCISE
Walking Meditation

Initially, while still sitting on your cushion, make a simple movement, like moving your hand in a wave. As the hand is moving, experience the movement — the feeling of air on the palm, the touch of fabric on the wrist. There is movement, nothing else. Make the movement, stop within it, and inhabit it a few times in this manner.

Going further, a traditional way of taking our meditation into movement is called walking meditation. Here we simply walk back and forth in a straight line, hands held together either in front of or behind us. We can set up a simple path — perhaps ten steps in length. Initially we are standing still at one end of it. We stop. All there is, is the sensation of standing there. As we stand, we can mentally say: *standing, standing, standing,* to advert our attention to our body.

After a moment we begin to move. We notice the intention, and then the activation in our legs. Our weight shifts onto one foot as the other foot bends forward onto the toes and then begins to rise. *Intending, intending, shifting, shifting, bending, bending, rising, rising.*

Our weight is now firmly on the other foot, and the foot in the air now moves forward and then begins to lower to touch the floor in front of us. *Moving, moving, lowering, lowering, touching, touching.*

The foot now settles back to become flat, placed firmly on the floor, and the weight shifts onto it. *Placing, placing, shifting, shifting.*

Our weight now shifted, the other foot begins to bend and then lifts and moves forward. *Bending, bending, lifting, lifting, moving, moving.*

It then lowers, touches the floor, and is placed, distributing our weight equally on both feet. *Lowering, lowering, touching, touching, placing, placing.*

So we have taken one step. We continue with the ten or so steps until the end of our pathway, then we bring both feet together and turn. *Turning, turning, turning.*

Then we start again.

Do this for three minutes, or longer if you like.

Moving without "Me"

We have taken steps with no "I" there, only movement. It is relaxing to inhabit our body in this manner. It's such a nice feeling. Enjoy this feeling of inhabiting yourself. Just do that. Inhabit you. Make a movement and inhabit it.

We can do this not only in walking meditation but also in the simple awareness of the whole body of the breath. We simply stop in that observation. In that stopped state, we can still be moving. We grow in the realization that we can move while we are mentally stopped. Our awareness of movement is singular; the movement and the awareness are one thing. It is not that we are aware of our movement from another vantage point, as if we were somewhere else. Our movement is present. It's actually here. We are embodied.

Questions and Comments

I was trying to be aware of what I was doing, but I found myself just freezing.

You could say it is a bit like landing a plane. We're up there on our meditation cushion, and we want to bring our flying cushion down into our lives. To do that we have to systematically explore the re-embodiment of our experience. We normally live by referring to a map of our experience rather than living in our experience without the map. When we have no map, our reactions are spontaneous and unplanned by us; this feels deeply disconcerting because we are attached to the security the map gives us. Indeed, our whole sense of identity is based in the map. So we have a scary sense of being out of control. We're not quite sure what we're going to do next.

This is why we take baby steps. We take this *vipassana* into a controlled environment — moving off the safety of our cushion into a simple movement, like our walking meditation. As this becomes familiar, we realize that our fears are without foundation. The foundation we thought we needed, the security of a map in which we "know" what we are doing, is not a fixed requirement. This brings a strange sensation. It is the equivalent of a caged animal suddenly realizing that the door to the cage has been left open. They sniff around the entrance, surprised and a little cautious that the bars are not there.

We are in that situation. But we can take our *vipassana* into actuality and make that the final phase of our practice. And if we're successful doing that, we'll end up with a practice we can do 24/7. We no longer have to do three minutes of meditation each day. We can start popping into meditation in whatever we're doing. We suddenly have a flexible Swiss Army knife of meditation techniques that can be used in any circumstance.

Would you say that the ability to practice in this ongoing, spontaneous manner is what is traditionally called pliancy or flexibility?

Yes. It is the union of *shamata* and *vipassana*. The fruit of *shamata* is pliancy. The fruit of *vipassana* is insight. We practice *shamata* to become flexible. Mental flexibility is the perfect foundation for insight. Mere concentration makes an inflexible foundation. If concentration is all we have, everything that arises and changes will cause us to lose our insight. We get shoved off our perch because we cannot respond in a flexible manner. But once we find our base of *shamata*, on that flexible foundation calm clarity can grow without limit.

Traditionally, supposedly you must sit for hours in *shamata* before you have a chance to attain pliancy. Will I have to build up the time gradually beyond the three-minute sessions?

If you can remain mindful for a week you can become enlightened! This surprising statement comes from the canonical writings of the Sattipathana Sutta within one of the main traditions of meditation. We can accumulate this capacity over time, like a dripping tap fills a bath. As long as it keeps dripping, it will fill the bath. Our three-minute sessions are accumulating pliancy in this manner. The problem of sitting longer is that we drift into the *idea* of sitting, at which point we are accumulating nothing, really. Our path is the path of *sugata*, the ease of calm clarity where insight comes to us as an endless vista of freedom.

Only read on once you have done
your seven days!

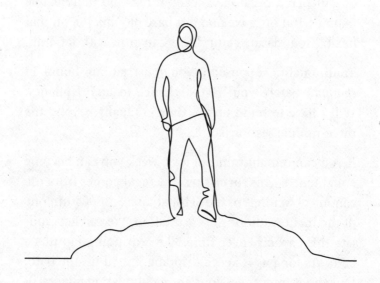

Postscript

Homo sapiens.

Knowing being. This is the enigmatic core of our experience: How can we both *be* and *know* at the same time?

We come into a world that is already in progress. From our earliest moments, our remarkable knowing capacity, this *sapiens* aspect of our humanity, accumulates ideas and associations from our experience and develops an increasingly sophisticated map of what we might meet in our travels. This map also contains deep memories and reflexes, generated by our growing up and made of all we have learned, both good and bad.

It is a map made of labels, shorthands that anchor our current experience to our memory of prior events. We continue to learn from our experience by creating additional shorthands, those labels we attach to things and events, and storing them away so they are ready to be applied to what might happen to us in the future. Through this process we can access how it went last time and therefore modify our behavior in the light of our previous experience. While many animals can do this to some extent, we are by far the most versatile at this, and humans have dominated all other species as a result. Learning from experience is fundamental to us. Since the primary characteristic of such an activity is the ability to label the present in the light of the past, it is inherently circular. This brings all kinds of consequences that we need to understand, for if our past prefigures our present, in a very real sense we are indeed trapped, held in a prison of our own cognition.

There is probably a strong genetic component to this as well. A fundamental paranoia appears to be hardwired into our cognition, possibly arising from when humans were living in the Serengeti being prowled by saber-toothed cats. It's why bad news is newsworthy, and good news is not. Bad news captures our attention, because our mapmaking capacity has a protective function and reacts to it instantly. It is almost as if it triggers an internal voice that asks, "Is there something I need to fix?" On the other hand, good news is merely safe information, so who cares? Needless to say, when you look at social media, newspapers, or news feeds, they are full of bad news. This is what interests our mapmaker. But this persistent flow of potential problems causes us to become exhausted by current events, pulled this way and that, almost as if we can't control the reactivity we're being subjected to.

Further to this, there is another element of this map of labels we need to understand. The labels merely represent, but do not replace, the sensations they are based on. Indeed, some of the labels that seem so central to our lives, such as the personal pronouns that place us in our memory of events, or the markers of time that allow us to construct coherent narratives around what happened, are not present in actuality at all. This realization opens to us a way of addressing deep questions concerning personhood and time in a novel and incisive way.

So what can a three-minute daily practice for fourteen weeks do to address this situation? If you are reading this, having taken this journey, I hope you will agree that it can do a lot. By developing a calm base, we can reduce reflexive reactivity, calm shattered nerves, and become more balanced in the face of what confronts us. And then we begin to see clearly. This capacity to see clearly is our birthright. It is not so much that it needs to be developed, like the skill to overcome reactivity that is the central theme of our *shamata* practice. Rather, our clear seeing has always been with us, but requires the calm flexibility of *shamata* to give it a stable base.

What is meditation? Seen from this perspective, it is an art. *Vipassana* is an art, the art of living that we develop once we have become comfortable in our own skin. If we can understand our own perception, and success-fully overcome the basic reactivity that we all experi-ence, our life can become a creative display instead of a prison. But as long as we do not understand how we make the world, our mapmaking has the potential to limit us, holding us tight in the prison of the past, from moment to moment.

Once our reactivity lessens, the continuous narrative, the claustrophobic container in which we have lived all these years, becomes visible. We realize that the cage that constrains us is of our own making. Through our meditation we learn to move, cautiously at first but then with increasing confidence, into another way of being, a freedom that is not continuously narrated by our mapmaker as if our life is being lived by someone else. We can learn to extend this experience with other skills, some of which are pointed to below. But this journey is our own. It's up to us. With our daily three minutes, we have begun.

Continuing the Journey

It would be wonderful, but somewhat naive, to expect that the writings in this book would form the end of the story, and that from then on the happy reader would simply figure out their own meditation practice. The insights presented point in that direction, for certain. However, our reflexive mapmaking is not going to be so easily overcome.

The key to our success is persistence, but for persistence to be stable it must be based on firm intent. If our three-minute sessions have shown us anything, it is that we are indeed embedded in a display, but that display can be seen, and it is possible to act without giving the display itself automatic dominance over our choices. If these realizations inform our outlook, then we can develop a firm intent to explore further.

To develop further we should stabilize and enhance what we have learned. We could say we have become "meditators." Go into any bookstore, and there are shelves of books on the subject. There are also thousands of organizations offering advice and practice, all the way from mindfulness-based stress reduction (MBSR) courses, to ten-day silent *vipassana* retreats, to lying flat at the end of yoga classes, to extended stays at dedicated meditation centers, to mindful prayer, to learning inner tennis or inner golf — the list is a long one.

The key for three-minute meditators is that the path we choose and the choices we make are embodied ones. We don't want to read about a technique or approach without embedding what we read in experience, for otherwise we only accumulate ideas. It is good to be open to learning new techniques, to find fruitful places to embody our experience. Our intuition can become powerful once we release it from the mapmaking constraints it otherwise operates within.

So keep practicing. Repeat the entire three-minute progression if you like, or choose one of the exercises to make into a daily practice. Three minutes is fine, but if you find yourself extending it, of course that is fine too! The key at this stage is to keep going, and journal about it. Write down impressions and realizations, noting what came most naturally or felt most helpful. If suggestions come to you, intuitions or ideas of what you might find out or do, write them down too and always act on them. If we take up suggestions that come to us in this way, we empower what we are doing and send a strong message to ourselves that we want to develop further. This encourages more suggestions and activates our innate intelligence to free itself from the cage of ideas in which it has been imprisoned. In no time we will forge our own way.

During the course of a busy day, we often find ourselves feeling out of sorts or flustered. Here a simple rapid reset can work wonders. Just for a moment, be aware of touch. As in the breath meditation in chapter 3, turn to the feeling of your body as you sit on a chair, or the touch of your fingers on something you pick up, or, of course, the breath itself. Ten seconds is enough. This is not to enter some absorbed state of meditation as if we were retreating into a castle; it is to establish a break in the momentum of events, however small. That small break is a reset, a chance to recenter, to create a little gap in the relentless flow of reflexive reactivity. So much of what we do is in a chain — one thing leading to another. Even a small break allows us to turn in a different direction. A small break can have big results!

Some people find themselves drawn to longer sessions, even to visit dedicated meditation centers for periods of intensive practice. This is wonderful, but not all of us have the means, inclination, or time to do this. Thankfully, such visits are not a requirement for moving forward in our practice. My own personal training has followed a three-step process: reading about a technique or approach, running it over in my mind to check I really understand it, and then applying it in practice. For example, we might read about reflexive reactivity, understand how it arises when impressions appear at one of the sense gates, and experience how a calm base defuses it as it arises. This kind of practical empowerment is what I hope has come through the pages of this book.

Meditation is not difficult. Actually, it is a not doing. A not doing is neither difficult nor easy. Since it is neither one nor the other, we simply settle in and do it anyway, just for three minutes. The directness of that intention has its own clarity. It is its own reward.

For anyone interested in
exploring the three-minute
approach in more detail, classes are
given twice a year at Dharma College
(www.dharma-college.com).
We also offer one-year classes based
on a more detailed examination of
our cognitive function, and many
other classes as well.
Check it out!

Glossary

nivarana   a hindrance or obstacle to practice, of which there are five: agitation, dullness, attraction, aversion, and doubt.

samadhi   perfect concentration, or in some traditions, perfect intuitive awareness.

shamata   calmness meditation geared toward non-reactiveness.

sugata   blissful effortlessness or relaxed awareness.

sukha   happiness.

trataka   focusing on one sense gate to the exclusion of the others.

vicara   the ability to savor the object of our attention; the second phase of concentration.

vipassana   clear seeing.

vitaka   the faculty of mind that enables us to pay attention to something; the first phase of concentration.

Acknowledgments

The publication of this book has been possible through the assistance and enthusiasm of Duncan Baird, a good friend and an ex-publisher who took one of my courses and helped me polish the text. Richard Zeiss created the transcripts from the original class recordings.

Duncan also found in New World Library an excellent publisher willing to take it on. I wish to offer many thanks also to all the staff there, particularly Kristen Cashman, managing editor, whose incisive editing and careful questions helped me to clarify the text; and Jason Gardner, executive editor, who acquired the book for publication and offered invaluable aid throughout the publication process. I also want to thank Kim Corbin, senior publicist, who led all the publicity and social media, and all the other staff at New World Library for helping to bring this book into being.

Finally I would like to thank all my students at Dharma College and worldwide for providing the inspiration to clarify thoughts and set things clearly; and my wonderful wife Wangmo, who remains a steadfast inspiration to everyone who has the good fortune to meet her.

About the Author

Dr. Richard Dixey is a scientist and lifelong student of Asian philosophy. Holding a PhD in biophysics and an MA in the history and philosophy of science, he directed the Bioelectronic Research Unit at St. Bartholomew's Hospital in London before becoming CEO of his own biotechnology company, Phytopharm Plc. In 2007 he moved to California to devote himself to deepening his own practice and running the Light of Buddhadharma Foundation in India with his wife Wangmo, the eldest daughter of the well-known Tibetan lama Tarthang Tulku. A senior faculty member at Dharma College in Berkeley, a school dedicated to re-envisioning Asian wisdom traditions for a contemporary audience, he divides his time between California and India.